B. Chirva

SOCCER
Basic elements of zonal pressing tactics

2016

УДК 796 332
Ч 64

Ч 64 **Chirva B.** Soccer. Basic elements of zonal pressing tactics. – Moscow, 2016. – 76 с.

ISBN 978-5-98724-191-2

This monograph presents particular provisions of soccer teams defending tactics with the use of zonal pressing.

Highlighted are typical local situations involving one-two defending players specific to different tactical schemes of play construction by teams applying zonal pressing.

Individual actions and cooperation of players from the defending team in these situations representing basic elements of zonal pressing tactics are considered.

УДК 796 332
Ч 64

ISBN 978-5-98724-191-2

CONTENTS

INTRODUCTION

Comparative analysis of teams of high proficiency in mid-90s of the 20 century, that built their defense crucially in different ways, has shown those who employed a zonal method of defending actions organization conceded roughly by 50 per cent less goals compared to teams that used man to man marking and libero.

Later at the turn of 21 century almost all over the world in football there was transition to building of defending actions according to the zonal method.

It should be noted that zonal method of defense has been already used a few decades ago, but at the modern stage of football development it came up with a new content which consists in its conversion to so called zonal pressing.

Zonal pressing is understood to be dynamic and powerful pressure on a player from the attacking team, who tries to take possession of the ball or already possessing it, put by players from the attacking team individually and together in one or another pitch zones depending on a situation, when they are situated initially and act according to provisions of zonal method of defense.

Zonal pressing suggests depriving the opponent of time and space for actions with the ball due to the ball location and opportunities of its delivery by players from the attacking team to one or another area of the pitch.

It is based on footballers' anthropometric, motive and technical capabilities to block one or another space in size across the width and length individually and in interaction with each other, situating differently.

In the context of whole team formations, providing realization of zonal pressing, there are specific tactical techniques of individual and group actions of players from the defending team.

On one hand, these actions and interactions are typical to different tactical schemes of play construction by teams applying zonal pressing, and on another, they completely differ from actions and interactions of defending players while man to man marking.

Hence knowledge about how footballers should act in typical in terms of zonal pressing situations offers an opportunity firstly to coach players with these actions intentionally using specific drills, secondly to adjust footballers' tactical individual and group actions directly during the game, and thirdly to apply different schemes of team play organization in the context of zonal pressing tactics.

Legend keys presented in fig. 1 are used in describing footballers' actions in this book.

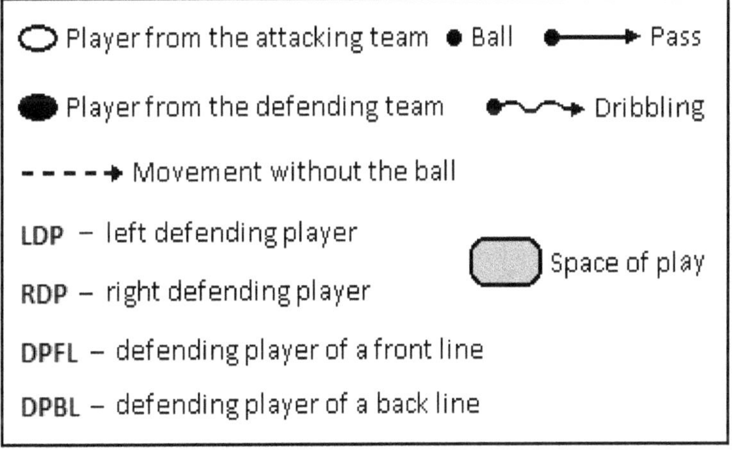

Fig. 1. Legend keys used in describing footballers' actions

For notes

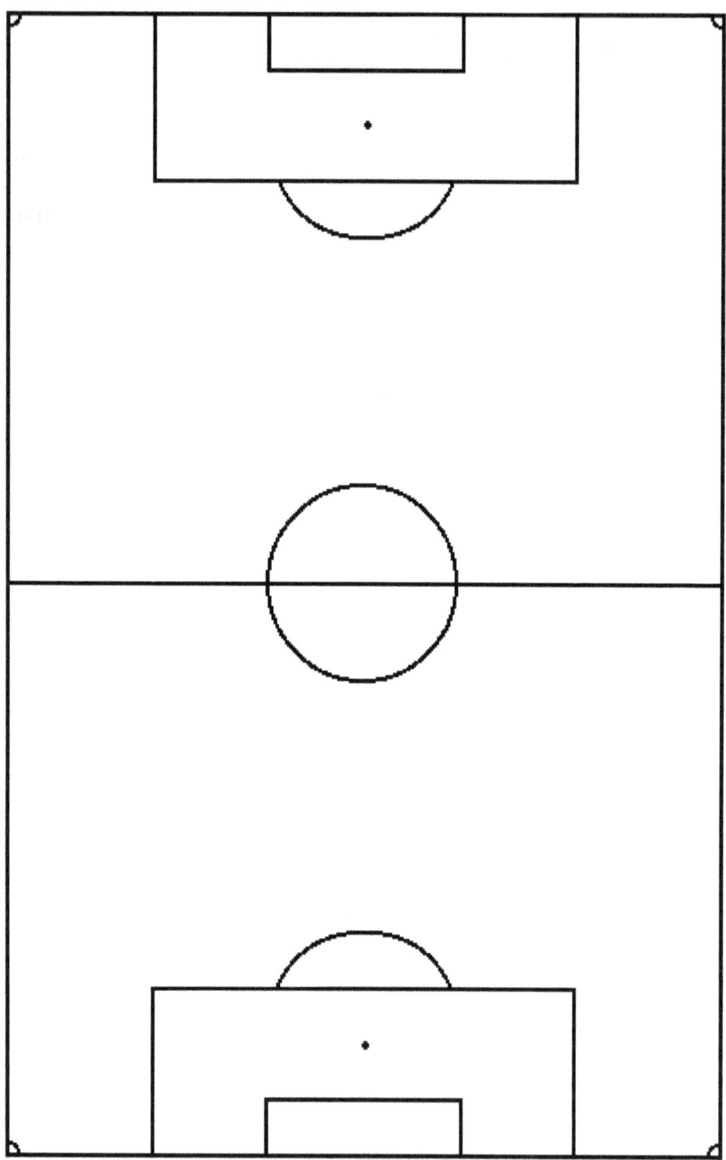

CHAPTER 1. KINDS OF TYPICAL LOCAL SITUATIONS IN DEFENCE WHILE USING ZONAL PRESSING INSIDE OF DIFFERENT TACTICAL SCHEMES OF PLAY

Zonal pressing may be realized with various tactical schemes of team play organization (with different correlation of players from different «play lines», different players' position relative to each other in «play lines», different number of «play lines»).

From the perspective of raising of defending actions efficiency in this regard at least two questions are raised:

– firstly, how footballers should act in defense in various situations performing zonal pressing in the context of definite tactical scheme of team play building;

– secondly, do actions of defending players change in principle in case of team's transition to use of zonal pressing in the context of another tactical scheme of play.

When considering game episodes with the involvement of sufficiently large number of players from the attacking and defending teams, it is hard to define which actions and interactions of defending players are of fundamental nature, and which are performed just ad hoc due, to variety of variants of play situations' development.

Therefore to answer questions above it is necessary:

– to mark out from different in duration and number of participating players play episodes such local situations, involving one or two defending players, that are specific to certain play schemes of teams applying zonal pressing;

– to conduct a comparison study of local situations, involving one or two defending players, specific to certain play schemes concerning if these local situations are typical while using zonal pressing in the context of another tactical play schemes.

Observing matches of teams of high qualification (participating in such tournament as World Cup, European Championship and European Cups) applying zonal pressing allowed defining the following.

First. There are several types of local situations in defense (fig. 2) typical of different tactical schemes of play construction (fig. 3-5):

– «one defending player on attacking player without the ball situated in front of him along the length of the pitch»;

– «one defending player on attacking player without the ball situated in front of him along the length of the pitch»;

– «two defending players on attacking player moving with the ball towards them along the length of the pitch»;

– «two defending players on attacking player without the ball situated between them along the length of the pitch».

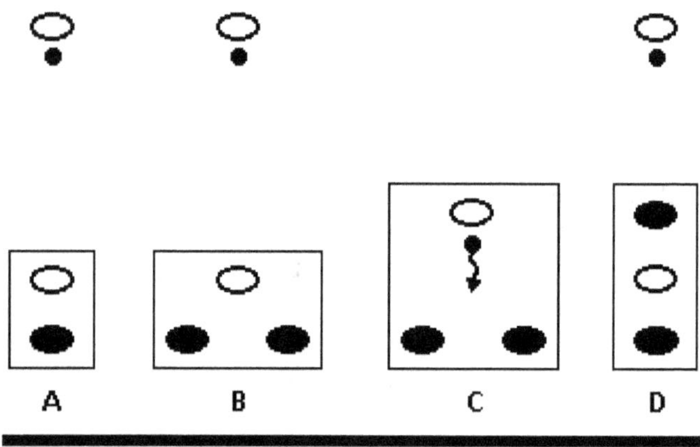

Fig. 2. Kinds of typical local situations involving one or two defending players occurring while using zonal pressing in the context of different tactical schemes of play

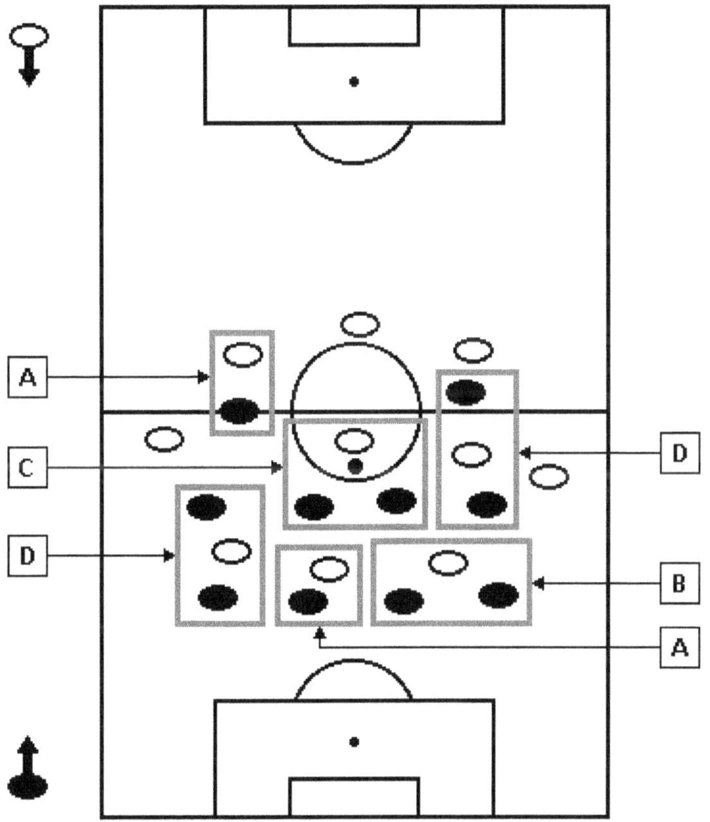

A – «one defending player on attacking player without the ball situated in front of him along the length of the pitch»;

B – «two defending players on attacking player without the ball situated between them along the length of the pitch»;

C – «two defending players on attacking player moving with the ball towards them along the length of the pitch»;

D –«two defending players on attacking player without the ball situated between them along the length of the pitch»

Fig. 3. Typical local situations in applying zonal pressing by the team using four defenders and four midfielders

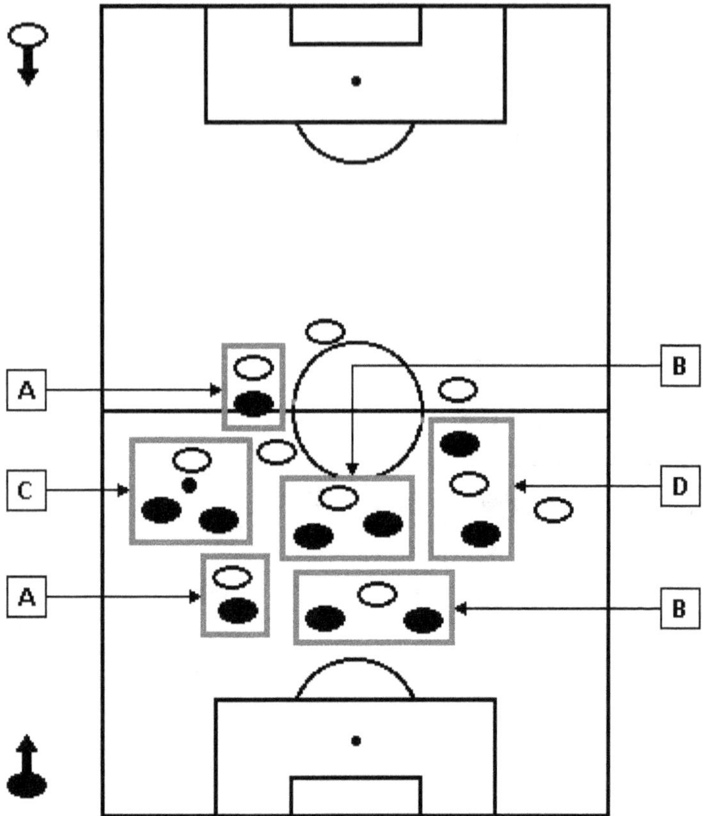

A – «one defending player on attacking player without the ball situated in front of him along the length of the pitch»;

B – «two defending players on attacking player without the ball situated between them along the length of the pitch»;

C – «two defending players on attacking player moving with the ball towards them along the length of the pitch»;

D – «two defending players on attacking player without the ball situated between them along the length of the pitch»

Fig. 4. Typical local situations in applying zonal pressing by the team using four defenders and five midfielders

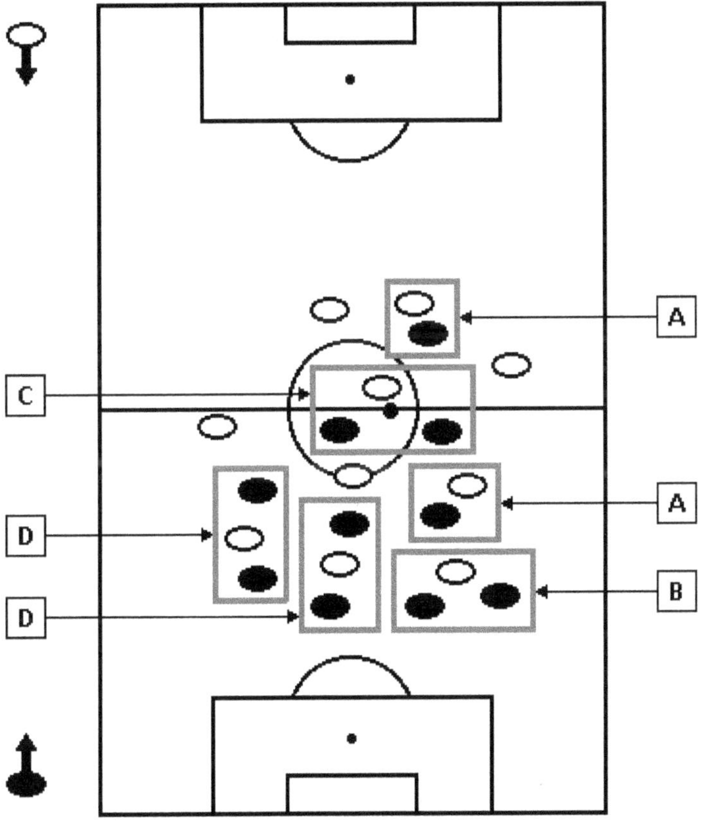

A – «one defending player on attacking player without the ball situated in front of him along the length of the pitch»;

B – «two defending players on attacking player without the ball situated between them along the length of the pitch»;

C – «two defending players on attacking player moving with the ball towards them along the length of the pitch»;

D – «two defending players on attacking player without the ball situated between them along the length of the pitch»

Fig. 5. Typical local situations in applying zonal pressing by the team using four defenders and three midfielders

Second. Actions of players from the defending team in each of listed above typical local situations are effectively the same in different tactical schemes of play construction.

This suggests that individual actions and interactions of two defending players in these situations present basic elements of zonal pressing tactics.

The following are detailed description of defending players' actions in typical local situations specific to different tactical schemes of play of teams applying zonal pressing.

For notes

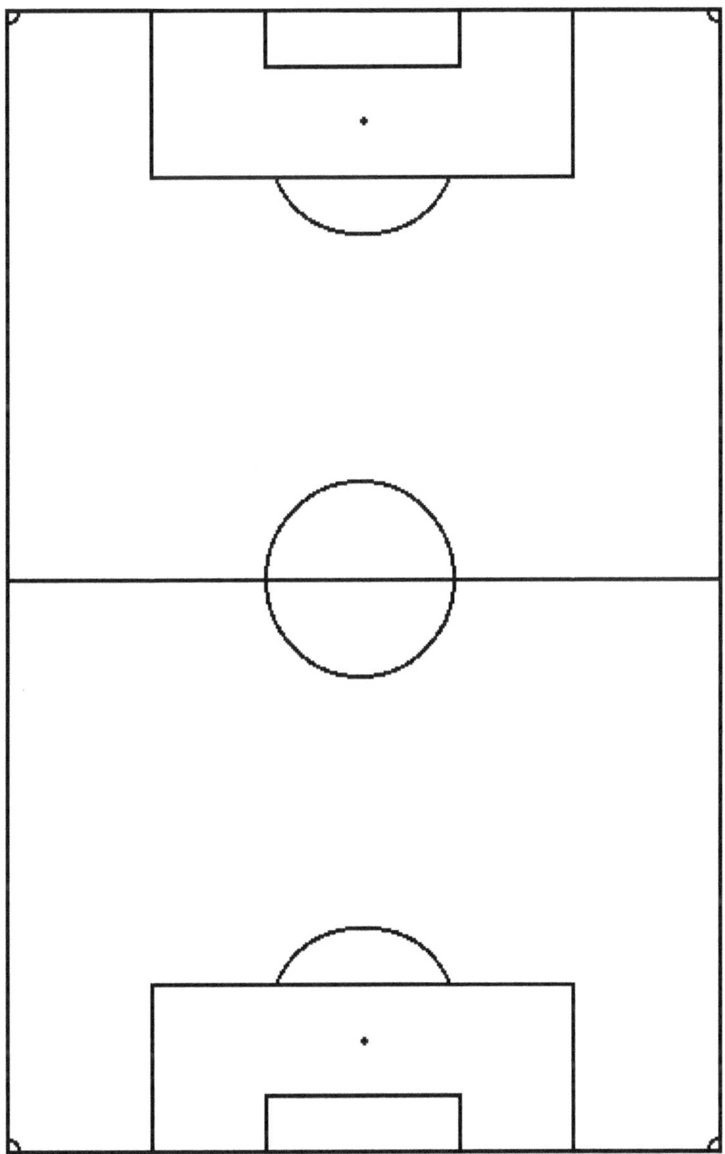

CHAPTER 2. DEFENDING PLAYERS' ACTIONS IN «ONE ON ATTACKING PLAYER WITHOUT THE BALL SITUATED IN FRONT OF HIM ALONG THE LENGTH OF THE PITCH» SITUATIONS

Introduction

One of basic elements of zonal pressing tactics are defending players' actions in «one on attacking player without the ball, situating in front of him along the length of the pitch» situations, suggesting:

– controlling an opponent in «one's zone of responsibility»;

– restraint of his attempts to come over the ball in space situated in front of defending player and behind him;

– pressing the attacking player out towards the half-way line, if play episode takes place on the defending team's half.

It should be noted that above mentioned kinds of actions are specific for play in defensive line, whereas such actions as controlling the attacking player in «one's zone of responsibility» and restraint of his attempts to receive the ball in space in front of defending player may be performed by players both in midfield and attacking lines during zonal pressing.

Defending player actions while controlling the attacking player without the ball in his «zone of responsibility»

Sufficient efficiency of defensive play may be achieved when it is necessary for certain players from the defending team to control the space, which length is up to 8-10 meters across the width of the pitch.

If attacking player without the ball appears in «zone of responsibility» of certain player from the defending team, this defending player locates at some distance between opponent and his own goal-line.

During attacking player's local movements across the width and length of the pitch in area, situated in front of defending player, the defending one should also move, trying to keep this distance and his opponent in front of him, situating face or half-sideways to opponent's goal-line (fig. 6).

Such actions of defending player allow him not only to control movements of attacking player in his «zone of responsibility», but also to see actions of attacking player's partner possessing the ball, and to correlate opportunities of these two attacking player to act in concert in one or another time point.

The last fact is very important, as defending player actions of restraint controlled by him attacking player attempts to receive the ball during zonal pressing are exactly built on the ground of assessment of character of this attacking player movements and availability of his partner, possessing the ball, to perform a pass.

For example while man on man marking the defending player at certain time points may be situated even back to attacking player possessing the ball, because he is in charge only for the certain opponent.

Therefore one of the key provisions of defensive play with the zonal pressing is that players from the defending team do not close with attacking player without the ball while controlling him

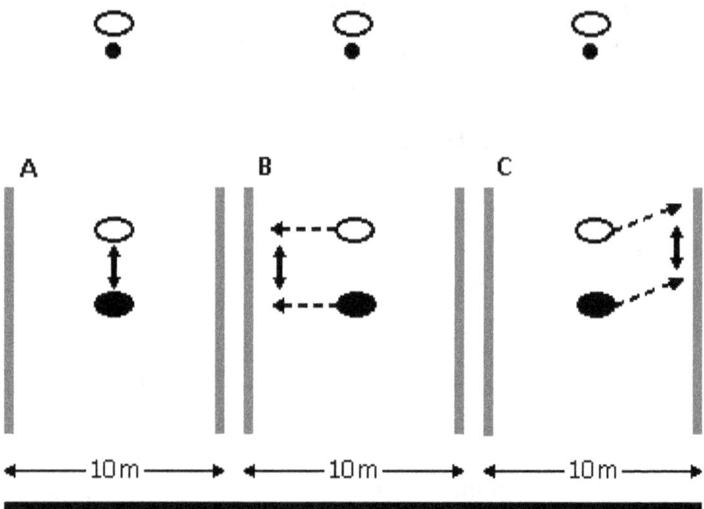

Fig. 6. Defending player's position and actions while controlling attacking player without the ball in his « zone of responsibility»

in their «zone of responsibility» until the ball is sent to him (as it is happened while man on man marking).

Otherwise they «open» the space behind their back, in which players from the defending team can deliver the ball straightaway by performing a pass (fig. 7).

The «gap» between defending and attacking players may be from 1 to 8-10 meters depending on their speed capabilities and on which area of the pitch they are situated in, on distance between attacking player and his partner possessing the ball.

Speaking about some average distance on which it is reasonably for the defending player to be situated from the attacking player while controlling him, it is about 3 meters.

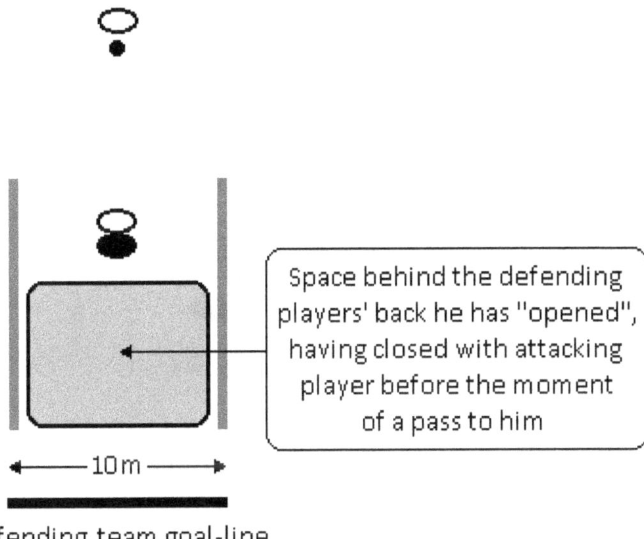

Fig. 7. Wrong in terms of zonal pressing position of defending player while controlling attacking player without the ball in his «zone of responsibility»

Such a «gap» between defending and attacking players is optimal for situations when attacking player's partner possessing the ball is situated 15-30 meters away from them, and defending and attacking players' «one on one» play episode doesn't take place in 18-yard box.

To answer the question why it is better for defending player to be approx 3 meters away from the attacking player while controlling him, it is necessary to consider attacking player's possible actions to receive the ball in the defending player's «zone of responsibility» and defending player's counteractions.

In this case in principle attacking player's actions of possessing the ball come down to attempts to receive it in space in front of defending player (at the foot) or behind his back (on a way) (fig. 8).

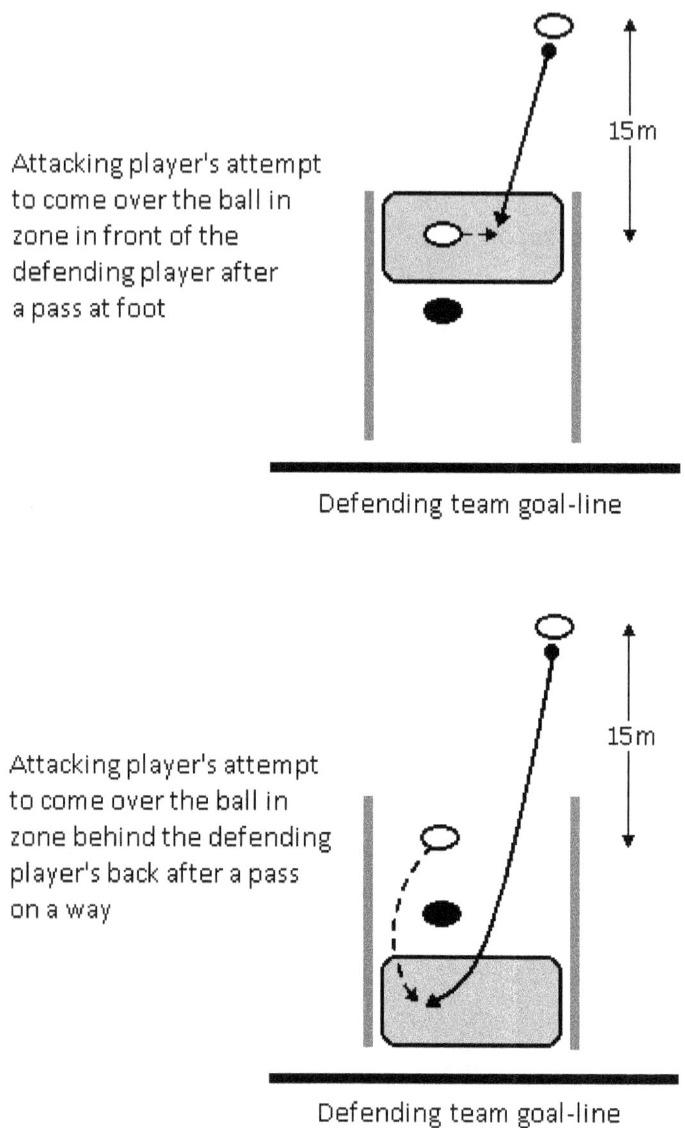

Fig. 8. Variants of attacking player's actions for receiving the ball in the defending player's «zone of responsibility»

Defending player actions while performing a pass at the attacking player's foot

While performing a pass at the attacking player's foot defending player abruptly goes at the attacking player and tries to intercept the ball or attack the opponent at reception of the ball, anticipating the moment and the direction of sending of the ball on the passing player's movements and entering into physical contact with him within the rules* (fig. 9).

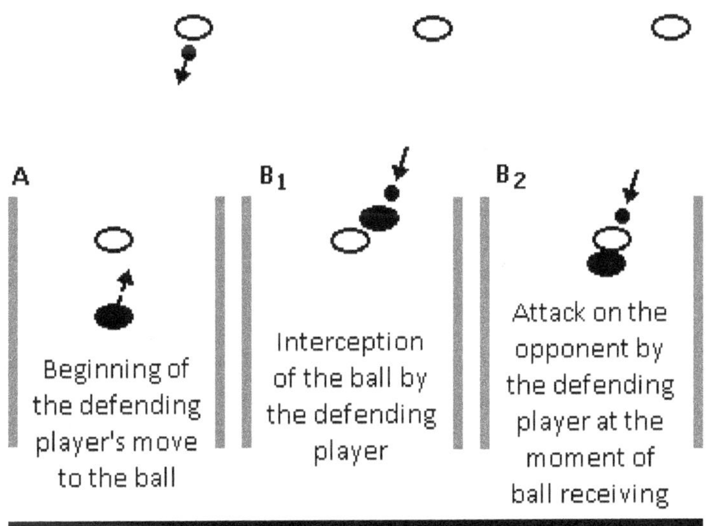

Fig. 9. Defending player's actions while performing a pass at the attacking player's foot during the zonal pressing

*While single combat for the ball Game rules permit:

– shoulder to shoulder push of the opponent possessing the ball;

– push to the opponent's permitted back region in case he blocks the ball.

Consequently defending player, unless intercepting the ball, forces attacking player to turn towards or sideways to his goal-line, lower his head for controlling the ball and worsen control of play situation, make a pass or begin to move with the ball back or across the pitch in conditions of physical contact.

Before sending the ball to the attacking player it is necessary for the defending player to be at such a distance from him in order to make it clear to partner of the attacking player, possessing the ball, that attacking player is free and the ball can be sent at his foot without risk, though in case of pass to the attacking player's foot to make it to play on the interception or tackle at the moment of opponent's reception of the ball in time.

When distance between attacking player and his partner possessing the ball is 15-30 meters, the fulfillment of these conditions can be exactly secured, if defending player is situated 3 meters away from the attacking player before the moment of sending the ball to him.

There may occur situations, when defending player, having defined the moment of sending the ball to the attacking player wrong, begins to go to the interception of the ball untimely, whereas a partner of the attacking player delays a pass performance. As a result, defending player turns out to be directly next to the attacking player, although a pass to this player didn't follow.

In this case defending player should «tear» the distance with the attacking player up and resume previous distance between them.

If it is followed with a pass to the attacking player's foot indeed, defending player should abruptly go at attacking player again, anticipating the moment of pass performance and its direction.

In situations when attacking player, managed to receive the ball despite pressing and control it for some time, has performed a pass, defending player should also start back quickly.

This is due to the fact that attacking player, having pass the ball to the partner, can quickly move into space behind the defending player's back and possess the ball sent by a partner with a first or second touch in it (fig. 10).

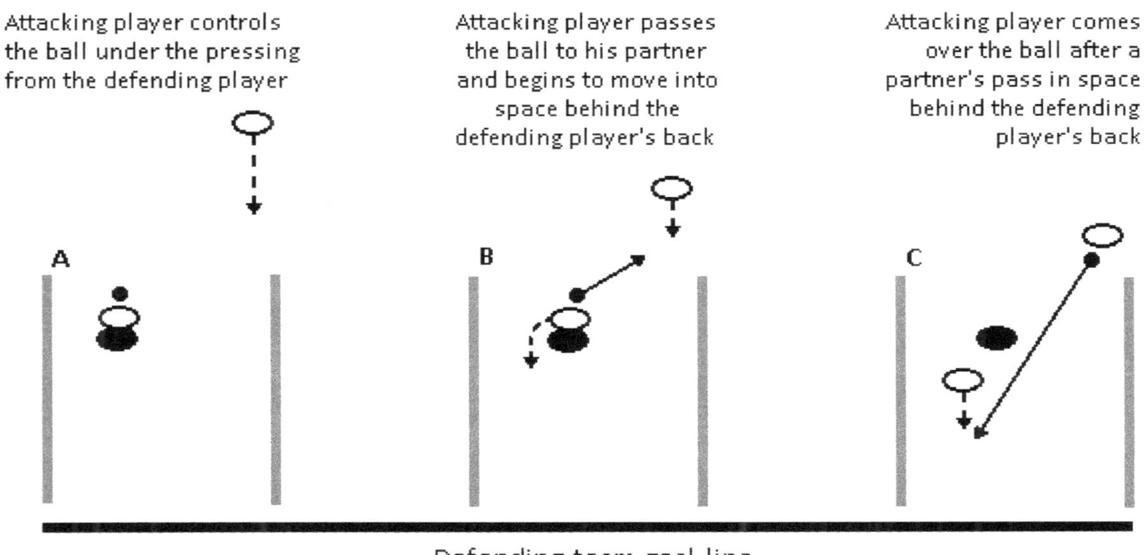

Fig. 10. Possible actions of players from the attacking team to deliver the ball into space behind the defending player's back, when attacking player managed to receive the ball at the foot under pressing from defending player

Defending player actions while performing a pass on the attacking player's way

In cases when attacking player begins to open for reception of the ball into space behind the defending player's back, moving forward or forward and to the side, while a partner of the attacking player possessing the ball is ready to pass the ball on his way, it is necessary for the defending player to begin to move back or back and to the side subsequently (fig. 11).

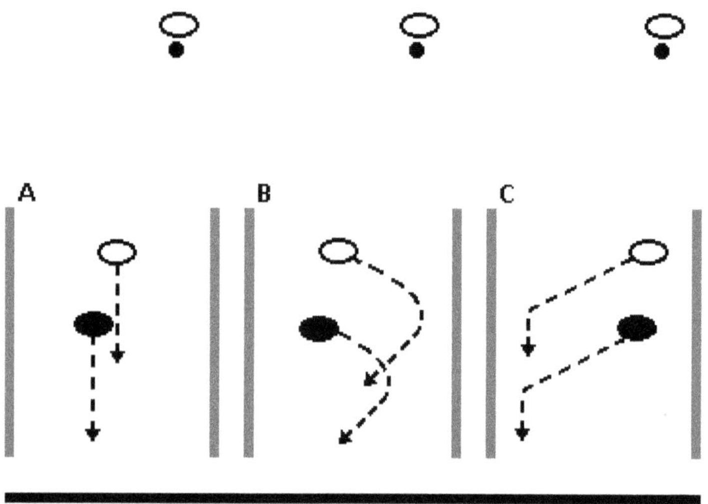

Fig. 11. Defending player's actions during the zonal pressing in situations when attacking player begins to move into space behind the defending player's back, while attacking player's partner possessing the ball is ready to pass it to him into this space

Ideally such actions of the defending player should be performed so that during sending the ball on the attacking player's way not only the possibility of him receiving the ball is excluded, but also situations when it depends on speed performance of attacking and defending players, who will get to the ball first.

With equal speed performance of defending and attacking players in case of sending the ball on the attacking player's way defending player can get to the ball first with sufficient cushion of time for error-free performance of following actions subject to the following.

First. Defending player should begin to move backwards timely and try to keep the «gap» of 3-4 meters between them before the moment of sending the ball to the attacking player.

This is possible with precise assessment of character and beginning of attacking player without the ball actions and preparative actions of his partner possessing the ball for pass performance, with quick reaction to their actions and fast performance of movement backwards.

Basically the distance between defending and attacking players before the moment of sending the ball on the attacking player's way may be more than 3-4 meters.

The more this distance, the less chances the attacking player has to receive the ball in space behind the defending player's back, even with advantage in movements speed.

However in case of big «gap» between defending and attacking players (8-10 meters) defending player may be late to attack an opponent in the moment of ball reception, if the one would suddenly stop, abruptly change the direction of movement to the opposite or to side, while partner would pass the ball at his foot.

Second. Until the moment when defending player determines the direction of the ball sent by a partner of the attacking player he should move so that to see both attacking player without the ball and actions of his partner possessing the ball.

To this effect he may be situated face or side to the opponent's goal-line depending on direction and speed of movement of attacking player without the ball and position of attacking player's partner possessing the ball.

Third. While possible changes of direction of attacking player without the ball movements into space behind the back of defending player until the ball is sent to him, corresponding changes in defending player's direction of movement should not lead to that he couldn't see actions of an opponent with the ball for some time.

It should be stressed that defending player's actions in situations when attacking player began to move into space behind the defending player's back, while his partner possessing the ball is ready to send the ball into this space, **do not basically suggest creating an offside.**

In case if in these situations defending player doesn't start back timely, but goes forward trying to catch the attacking player offside, such actions may be considered incorrect.

This is due to the fact that while creating offside defending player may be mistaken himself firstly, secondly there is a major risk of mistakes caused with the lack of coordination in defending player and his partners' actions, and thirdly the offside of attacking player may be count passive.

Cases of offside creation by defending player may occur in following situations.

Attacking player without the ball begins to move quickly into space behind the defending player's back, but his partner possessing the ball is not ready to give a pass: locates face to his goal-line; handled the ball uncomfortably for pass performance; lost control on play situation under opponent's pressing.

Then defending player, having seen during movement backwards that the ball cannot be passed to the attacking player at the moment, abruptly changes direction of movement to the opposite and goes a few steps out towards the half-way line.

Defending player's actions while pressing the attacking player out towards the half-way line

With proper actions of defending player in cases when attacking player begins to open for reception of the ball into space behind the defending player's back, while a partner of the attacking player possessing the ball is ready to pass the ball on his way, there may be two following variants of situation development.

First. If the attacking player's partner performs a pass on the attacking player's way, defending player should be first at the ball.

Second. If the attacking player's partner doesn't dare to perform such a pass, attacking player will get closer to the defending team goal-line, than before the start of this episode, not being offside.

In the second case defending player should deprive the attacking player of advantage ground, having moved him away from the goal-line. This may be achieved by means of defending player going out at some distance towards the half-way line and catching the attacking player offside, from whence the last will be forced to go back to space between the defending player and goal-line of attacking team for reception of the ball.

Pressing the attacking player by the defending player out towards the half-way line may be performed at the time when the ball cannot be sent towards the goal-line of defending team.

Otherwise a pass opposite to the defending player's movement on the attacking player's way is possible, whereas the last may not be caught offside.

If we consider the real game episodes, when the defending player may go out to the half-way line on necessary in each specific situation distance until the moment when:

– the ball goes from player from the defending team to player from the attacking team;

– the ball goes from one player from the attacking team to another;

– player from the attacking team possessing the ball is not ready to sent the ball towards the defending team goal-line (fig. 12).

A little earlier than the moment when moving ball appears near the player from the attacking team, who can send it into space behind the defending player's back, or when attacking player possessing the ball prepared himself for sending the ball into this space, defending player should stop moving forward and get ready to move backwards. This is due to two conditions.

Firstly, initially controlled by the defending player attacking player may step out from offside quickly, and then try to receive the ball once again in space situated behind the defending player's back.

Secondly, another player from the attacking team may begin to move from deep into space behind the defending player's back for reception of the ball (fig. 13).

If a defending player have seen that some of attacking players starts to open into space behind his back, while their partner possessing the ball is ready to send the ball into this space, it is necessary for him to begin to move back and be closer to his goal-line, than this attacking player, during that move.

In this case the attacking player would have small chances to receive the ball in space behind the defending player's back, and if a pass at his foot follows, the defending player will be able to attack him at the moment of the ball reception.

To define the moment when the move backwards should be started the defending player has to see actions of the attacking player trying to receive the ball on his way, and his partner possessing the ball, and appreciate their opportunities to act in concert.

Therefore availability of a player from the attacking team possessing the ball to send the ball to a partner who begins to move into the space behind the defending player's back answers for a signal for the defending player to begin to move back while pressing the attacking player out towards the half-way line.

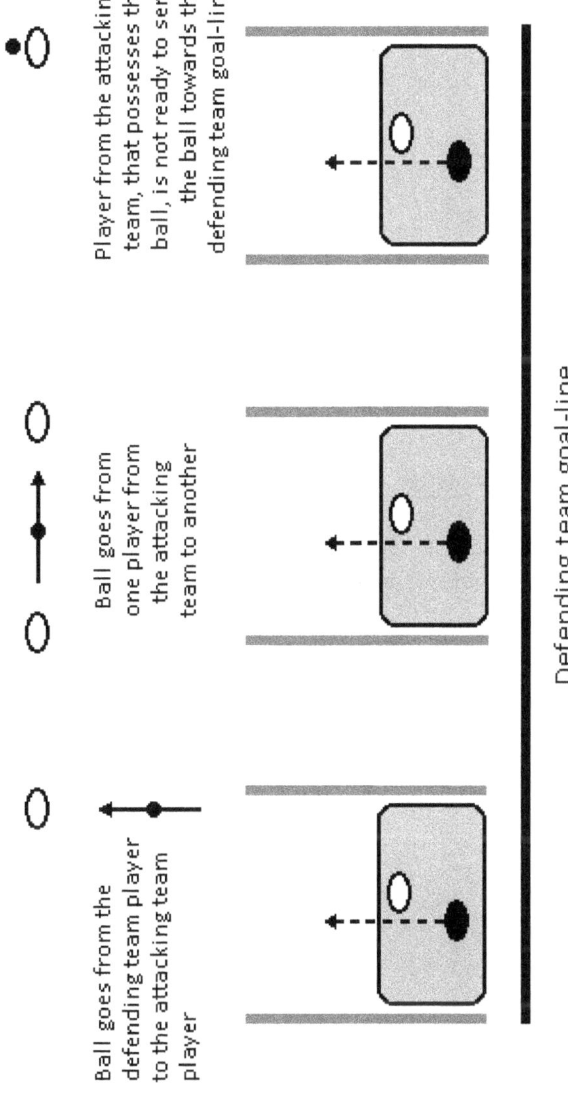

Fig. 12. Situations when a defending player may go forward to press the attacking player out towards the half-way line

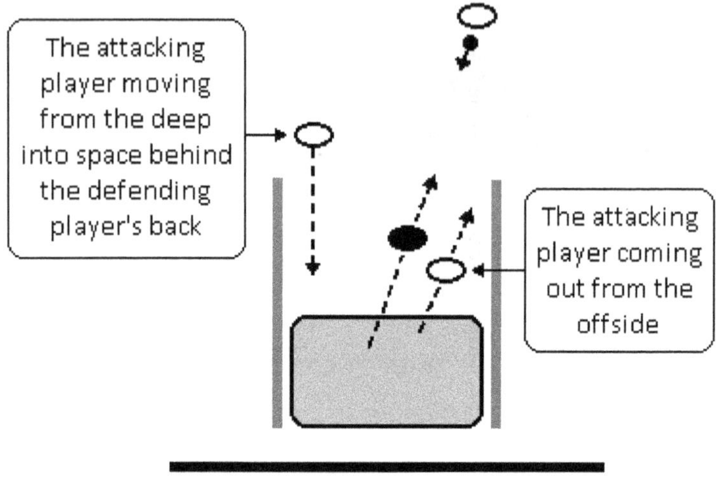

Fig. 13. Possible situation while pressing the attacking player out towards the half-way line by the defending player, when another attacking player begins to move from deep into the space behind the defending player's back, while the attacking player possessing the ball is ready to pass the ball on his way

Further actions of the defending player after he began to move towards his goal-line depend on direction of the ball sent to the attacking player. If a pass to the attacking player doesn't follow, the defending player may perform the pressing of an opponent out to the half-way line once again.

Resume

While constructing defensive play using the zonal pressing the defending player's countering to the attacking player without the ball in one on one situations suggests:

– controlling an opponent in «one's zone of responsibility»;

– restraint of the attacking player's attempts to come over the ball in space situated in front of defending player and behind him;

– pressing the attacking player out towards the half-way line, if play episode takes place on the defending team's half.

When performing these actions by the defending player it is essential to comply with the following provisions.

First. While controlling the attacking player without the ball in «zone of responsibility» it is necessary for the defending player to be at some distance from the opponent between him and his own goal-line until the moment of sending the ball to the attacking player.

The «gap» between defending and attacking players varies depending on situation, but basically it should be such that on one hand the attacking player's partner possessing the ball believes that the ball can be sent at the attacking player's foot without risk, and on another the defending player makes it to play on the interception or tackle at the moment of opponent's reception of the ball.

Second. While performing a pass at the attacking player's foot defending player abruptly goes at the attacking player and tries to intercept the ball or attack the opponent at reception of the ball, anticipating the moment and the direction of sending of the ball and entering into physical contact with him.

Third. If the attacking player begins to move for reception of the ball into space behind the back of the defending player, while the attacking player's partner is ready to pass the ball on his way, the defending player should begin to move back to eliminate a possibility of attacking player receiving the ball.

Fourth. To press the attacking player without the ball out towards the half-way line, the defending player should move around at some distance towards the half-way line and catch him offside, from whence the last will be forced to go back to space between the defending player and the goal-line of the attacking team.

Moving forward may be performed by the defending player at the moment when the ball cannot be sent by an opponent towards the goal-line of the defending team.

Fifth. The availability of a player from the attacking team possessing the ball to send the ball to a partner who begins to move into the space behind the defending player's back answers for a signal for the defending player to begin to move back while pressing the attacking player out towards the half-way line.

For notes

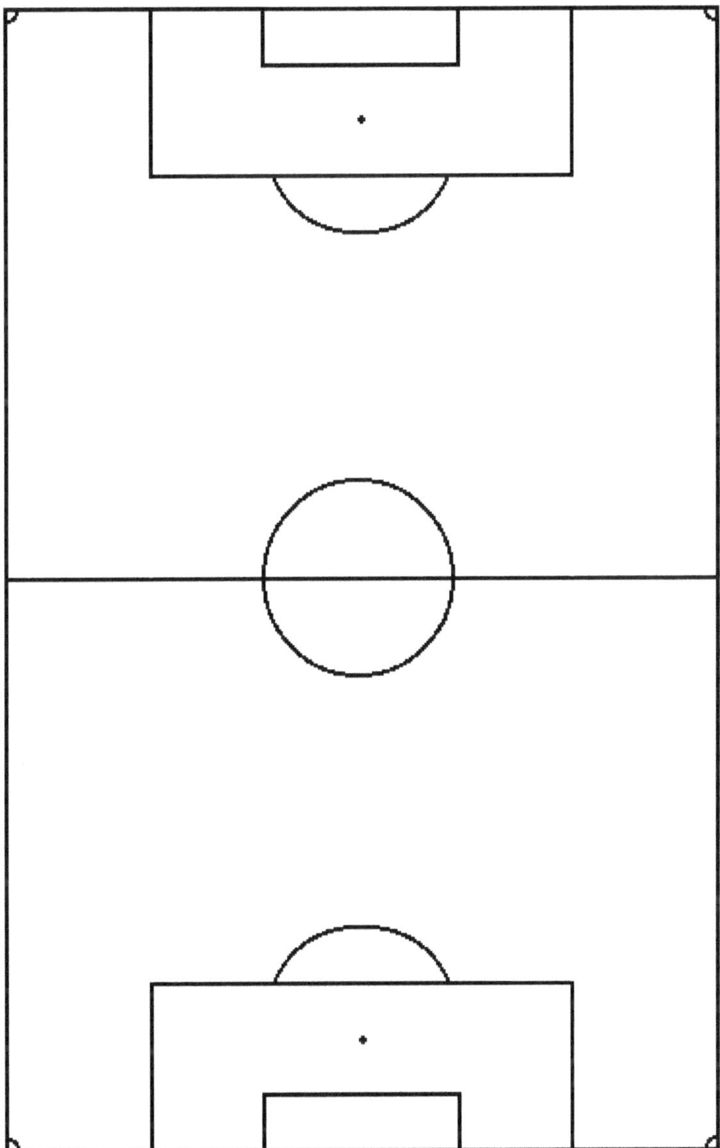

CHAPTER 3. DEFENDING PLAYERS' ACTIONS IN «TWO ON ATTACKING PLAYER WITHOUT THE BALL SITUATED IN FRONT OF THEM ALONG THE LENGTH OF THE PITCH» SITUATIONS

Introduction

In «one defending player on attacking player without the ball» situations attacking player can move along the length of the pitch for receiving the ball and overrun «zone of responsibility» of defending player, which is 8-10 meters across the width of the pitch at one point.

In these cases attacking player should occur in «zone of responsibility» of another defending player basically, as while constructing defensive play after the zonal manner two nearest to each other players of defending team and of one «play line» are situated roughly in parallel to each other along the length of the pitch at 7-10 meters.

If it happens, we can say that «one defending player on attacking player without the ball» situation transforms into «one defending player on attacking player without the ball plus one defending player, situating on the right or on the left of partner» situation.

Hence two defending players' tactics of play in «two defending players on attacking player without the ball, situating in front of them along the length of the pitch» situations suggests performance of actions exercised in «one defending player on one attacking player without the ball, situating in front of him along the length of the pitch» situations.

These actions include:

– controlling an opponent in «one's zone of responsibility»;

– restraint of his attempts to receive the ball in space in front of defending players (at foot) and behind them (on a way);

– pressing the attacking player out towards the half-way line, if play episode takes place on the defending team's half.

Besides of that, in «two defending players on attacking player without the ball, situating in front of them along the length of the pitch» situations there are definite interactions of defending players, specifically:

– «transfer» of the attacking player under partner's control in cases of this player switching from one defending player's «zone of responsibility» to another;

– choice of actions priority while restraint of attacking player's attempts to receive the ball at his foot;

– covering each other while one of them trying to intercept the ball sent to the attacking player, or take the ball away from the attacking player.

When considering defending players' actions in «two on attacking player without the ball, situating in front of them along the length of the pitch» situations, we mean the defenders play first, as all the specified kinds of defending players' actions in these situations are typical for the defensive play exactly.

With that certain actions of listed above may be performed both in midfield and defensive lines while constructing defensive play using zonal pressing.

Two defending players' actions while controlling the attacking player without the ball in their «zones of responsibility»

In cases when the attacking player without the ball appears in front of two defending players, they locate at 7-8 meters approx. parallel to each other across the width of the pitch and at some distance from the opponent between him and own goal-line.

During attacking player's local movements across the width and length of the pitch in the right or left defending player's «zone of responsibility» and his switches from one defending player «zone of responsibility» to another both defending players also move, trying to keep the distance between them at 7-8 meters and their opponent in front of them, situating face or half-sideways to the pitch (fig. 14).

Such actions allow them to control movements of attacking player in own and partner's «zone of responsibility», and also to see actions of attacking player's partner possessing the ball, and to correlate opportunities of these two attacking player to act in concert in one or another time point.

By analogy with how defending player, controlling an opponent in own «zone of responsibility» in «one on the attacking player without the ball», locates, it is better for two defending players to be approx 3 meters along the length from the attacking player without the ball while controlling him in their «zones of responsibility», providing that the play episode doesn't take place in the 18-yard box and that the attacking player's partner possessing the ball is situated at 15-30 meters from them.

Depending on the distance between the attacking player and his partner possessing the ball, attacking and defending players' speed capabilities and in what area of the pitch they are situated, the «gap» between attacking and defending player along the length of the pitch may vary.

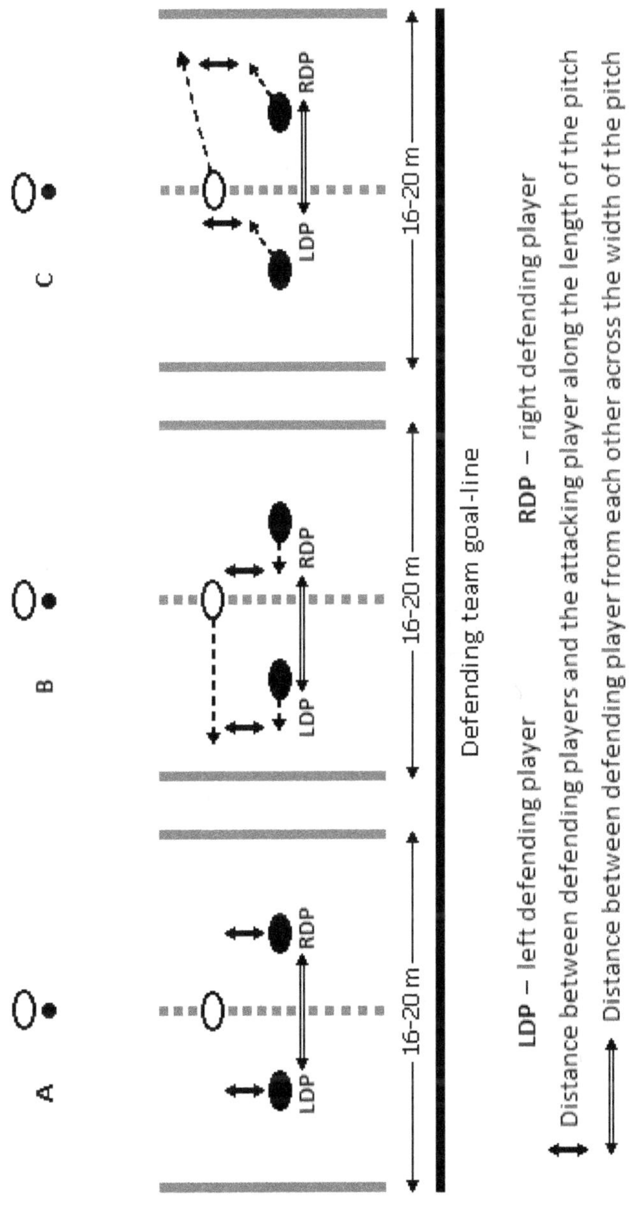

Fig. 14. Two defending player's position and actions while controlling attacking player without the ball in their «zone of responsibility» during the zonal pressing

Until the moment of a pass to the attacking player defending players do not close with attacking player for fear of «opening» the space behind their back and providing players from the attacking team with an opportunity to deliver the ball in this already uncontrolled space straightaway by performing a pass (fig. 15).

In this case in principle attacking player's actions of possessing the ball come down to attempts to receive it in space in front of defending players (at the foot) or behind their back (on a way).

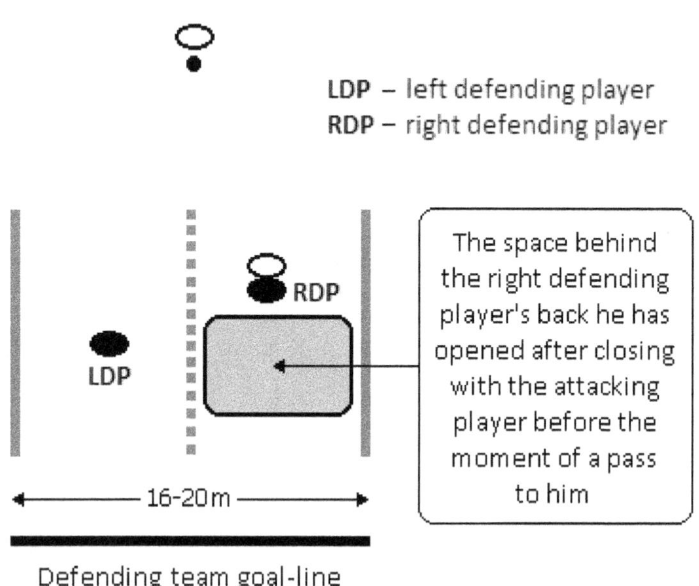

Fig. 15. Wrong in terms of zonal pressing position of either of defending players while controlling attacking player without the ball in his «zone of responsibility»

Two defending players' actions while performing a pass at the attacking player's foot

While performing a pass at the attacking player's foot one of two defending players acts the same as the defending player in «one on attacking player without the ball» situations while attacking player attempts to receive the ball at foot.

These actions present the following.

Defending player abruptly goes at the attacking player and tries to intercept the ball or attack the opponent at reception of the ball, anticipating the moment and the direction of sending of the ball and entering into physical contact with him within the rules.

Acting in such way the defending player either intercepts the ball, or forces attacking player to turn towards or sideways to his goal-line, lower his head for controlling the ball and worsen control of play situation, make a pass or begin to move with the ball back or across the pitch in conditions of physical contact.

Then one of defending players abruptly goes at the attacking player, another drifts towards the point, where the partner was situated before the moment of going at the attacking player, to «shut» the space left free.

The choice which of defending players has to go at the attacking player is due to in which area this player expects to receive the ball at foot.

This is due to that attacking player may plan to come over the ball in one of defending players «zone of responsibility», in which he was situated before sending the ball to him, and may move across the width of the pitch for receiving the ball into the other defending player's «zone of responsibility» just before a pass performance.

Any way it should the defending player, in whose «zone of responsibility» the attacking player tries to come over the ball, who goes on the attacking player in case of pass at his foot (fig. 16).

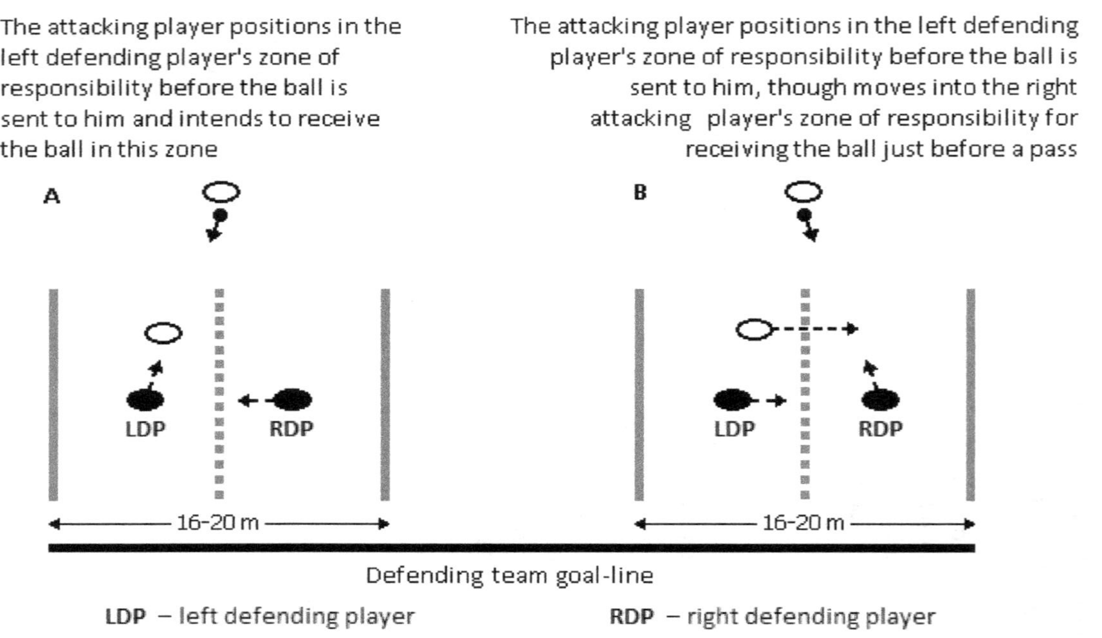

Fig. 16. Two defending players' actions during the zonal pressing while performing a pass at the attacking player's foot into one of defending players «zone of responsibility»

The most difficult for defending players is the defining of their actions priority while performing passes at the attacking player's foot when this player expects to come over the ball in area at the boundary of right and left defending players' «zones of responsibility».

In this case it is necessary to consider defending player's actions relating to definite play episode, as the choice which of them has to attack an opponent at the moment of him receiving the ball depends on specificity of play situation development, position and individual characteristics of footballers.

In principle there may be marked two provisions regarding the defining of two defending players' actions priority while performing passes at the attacking player's foot when this player expects to come over the ball in area at the boundary of right and left defending players' «zones of responsibility».

First. If two nearest across the width of the pitch players are central defenders (midfielders), then basically any of these players can go on the attacking player, though it is reasonably for those who is faster and plays better on the interception.

Second. If two nearest across the width of the pitch players are the full-back and the center-back (midfielders), then it is necessary for the center-back (midfielder) to go for interception, while full-back (winger) has to cover (fig. 17).

If the attacking player was able to receive the ball at foot, and then «leave» it after some time of possession, the defending player who has attacked an opponent has to start back quickly to the position he was on before going for interception.

In some cases the defending player pressing an opponent possessing the ball has to significantly change his position across the width of the pitch towards a partner relative to location area before the moment of going for interception.

Then, after the attacking player has performed a pass, it is reasonably for him to move back in area situated on the other side from the second defending player across the width of the pitch, whereby defending players finish an episode, having swap places with each other across the width of the pitch (fig. 18).

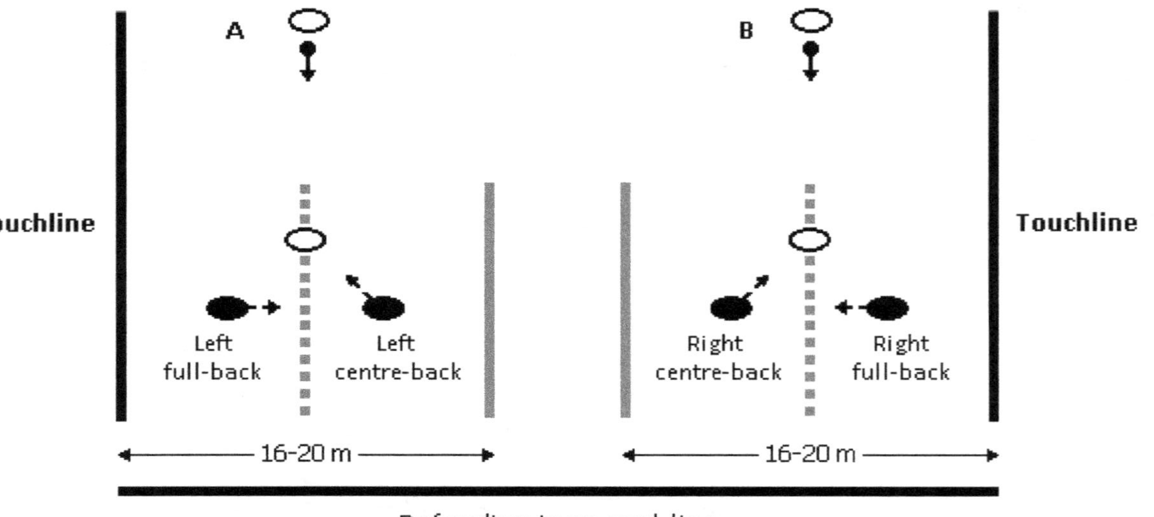

Fig. 17. Two defending players' actions during the zonal pressing while performing a pass at the attacking players foot into area at the boundary of their «zones of responsibilities», if they are full-back and center-back

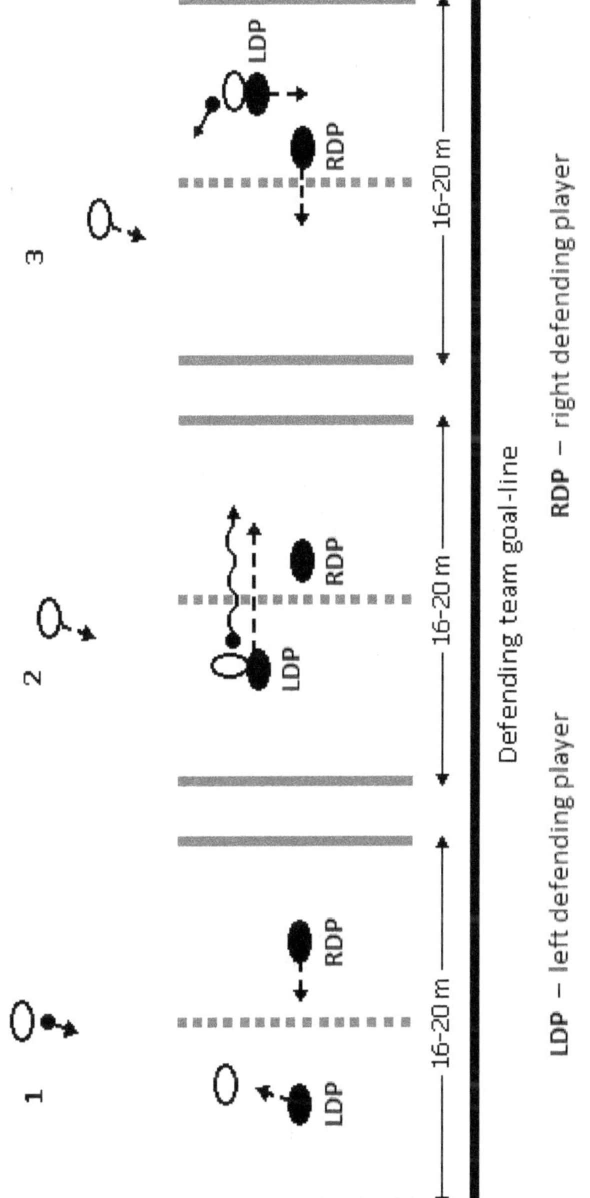

Fig. 18. Two defending players' actions during the zonal pressing, when one of them pressing an opponent, has significantly changed his position across the width of the pitch towards a partner relative to own location area, whereas the attacking player has performed a pass

Two defending players' actions while performing a pass on the attacking player's way

In cases when attacking player begins to open for reception of the ball into space behind defending players' back, moving forward or forward and to the side, while a partner of the attacking player possessing the ball is ready to pass the ball on his way, it is necessary for both defending players to begin to move back or back (fig. 19).

This is due to the fact that attacking player can move towards the area behind the back of one of defending players at first, but than change the direction of movement towards the area behind another defending player's back.

And if only the defending player, behind whose back the attacking player initially expected to come over the ball, starts back, it might be possible that the attacking player, having change the direction of movement, will receive the ball in the area behind whose defending player's back, who stayed put (fig. 20).

In those cases when the attacking player begins to move for receiving the ball into space behind defending players' back, their actions basically should be performed so that while sending the ball on the attacking player's way one of defending players gets to the ball first and with sufficient cushion of time. This is possible on the following conditions.

First. It is important for defending players to begin to move backwards timely and try to keep the «gap» of 3-4 meters between him and them before the moment of sending the ball to the attacking player.

To this effect it is necessary for them to anticipate development of situation (precisely appreciate the beginning of attacking player's without the ball actions and actions of the attacking player's partner possessing the ball) and perform moving backwards quickly.

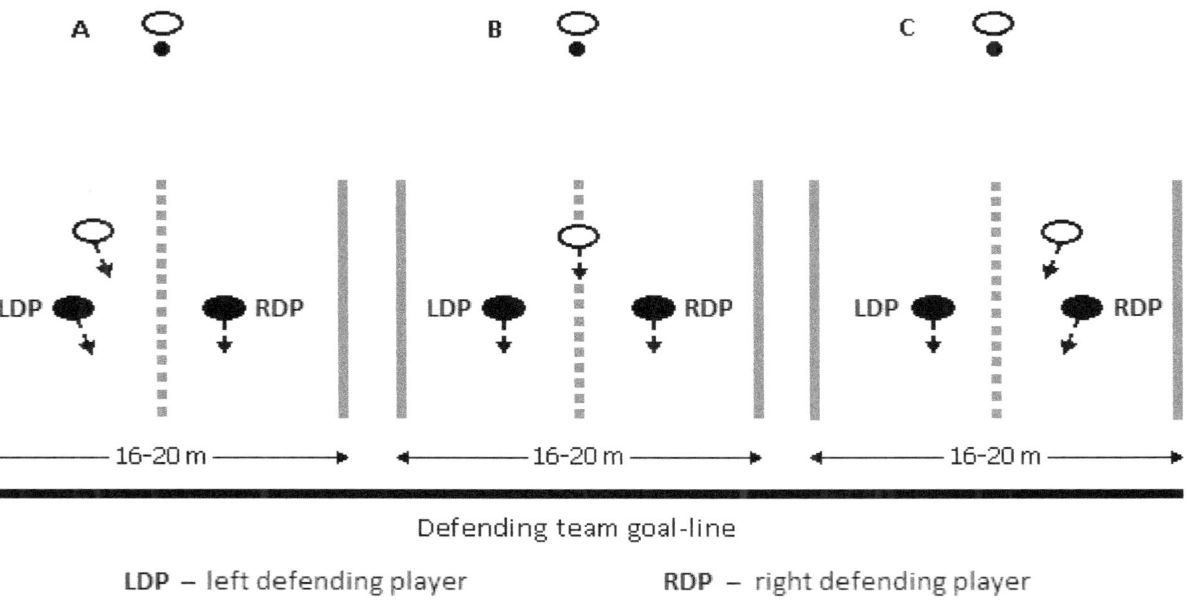

Fig. 19. Two defending players' actions during the zonal pressing before the moment of a pass to the attacking player, when this player begins to move into space behind their back

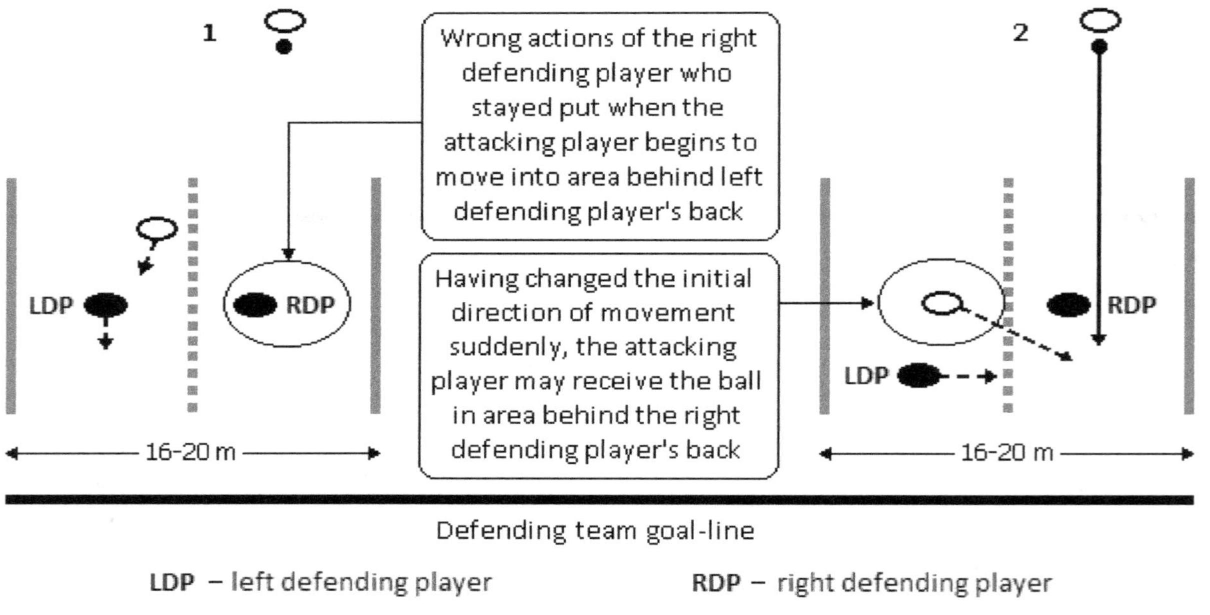

Fig. 20. Wrong in terms of zonal pressing actions of one of two defending players, when attacking player begins to move for receiving the ball into space behind the other defending player's back

In case of big «gap» between the attacking player and defending players (8-10 meters) the former has small chances to come over the ball in the area behind defending players' back, even overcoming them in speed of running, though defending players may be late to keep the attacking player from receiving the ball, if it is sent at his foot.

Second. Until the moment when defending players determine the direction of the ball sent by a partner of the attacking player they should move so (face or sideways to the pitch) that to see both attacking player without the ball and actions of his partner possessing the ball.

Third. While changes of direction of attacking player without the ball movement into space behind the defending players' back until the ball is sent to him, corresponding changes in defending players' direction of movement should not lead to that they couldn't see actions of the attacking player's partner for some time.

In situations then the attacking player has begun to open into space behind defending players' back, while his partner possessing the ball is ready to send the ball into this space, defending players' actions do not basically suggest creating an offside or non-performance of movement backwards.

This is due to the fact that in these cases there is a major risk of mistakes caused with the lack of coordination in defending players' actions, and the offside of attacking player may be count passive.

Defending players may create offside while the attacking player trying to receive the ball in space behind their back, **if while moving back they see the ball cannot be sent to this player at the moment.**

For example, the attacking player's partner possessing the ball locates face to his goal-line; lost eye control on the attacking player's actions, trying to get rid of the opponent's marking.

Two defending players' actions while pressing the attacking player out towards the half-way line

Proper actions of defending players in cases, when the attacking player begins to move into space behind their back, while his partner possessing the ball is ready to pass the ball on his way, may lead to that the attacking player's partner will scruple to perform such a pass. As a result the attacking player appears closer to the defending team goal-line, than he was before the beginning of this episode.

If play episode «two defending players on the attacking player without the ball» takes place on the defending team's half, when it is necessary for defending players to move the attacking player away from their goal-line by going at some distance towards the half-way line and catching him offside.

Pressing of the attacking player out towards the half-way line on necessary in each specific situation distance is performed under certain conditions, that require defending players to understand the situation development identically.

First. Defending players may go forward at the time when the ball cannot be sent towards their goal-line, specifically before the moment when:

– the ball goes from player from the defending team to player from the attacking team;

– the ball goes from one player from the attacking team to another;

– attacking player possessing the ball clearly isn't ready to perform a pass towards the goal-line of the defending team.

Second. While moving forward, defending players should try to observe a parallel arrangement relative to each other.

Third. A little earlier than the moment when it becomes possible to send the ball towards the goal-line of the defending team, defending players should stop going forward and get ready to move back.

This is due to the fact that the attacking player caught offside may quickly escape it and try to receive the ball in space behind defending players' back once more, or another player from the attacking team may begin to move from the deep for receiving the ball.

Fourth. Having seen that some of attacking players starts to open into space behind his back, while their partner possessing the ball is ready to send the ball into this space, defending players should begin to move back and be closer to their goal-line, than this attacking player, during that move.

Fifth. To define the moment of beginning of move backwards precisely, defending players have to see actions of the attacking player trying to receive the ball on his way, and his partner possessing the ball, and appreciate their opportunities to act in concert.

Resume

While constructing defensive play using the zonal pressing defending players' countering to the opponent in «two on attacking player without the ball, situating in front of them along the length of the pitch» situations suggests:

– controlling the attacking player in «one's zone of responsibility»;

– restraint of his attempts to come over the ball in space in front of defending players (at foot) and behind them (on a way);

– pressing the attacking player out towards the half-way line, if play episode takes place on the defending team's half.

In these situations defending players' interaction comes down to:

– «transfer» of the attacking player under partner's control in cases of this player switching from one defending player's «zone of responsibility» to another;

– choice of actions priority while restraint of attacking player's attempts to receive the ball at his foot;

– covering each other at attempts to intercept the ball sent to the attacking player.

While performing these actions it is necessary for defending players to comply with the following provisions.

First. While controlling the attacking player in own «zone of responsibility» before the moment of sending the ball to him it is necessary for defending players to locate at 7-8 meters approx. parallel to each other along the length of the pitch and at some distance from the opponent between him and own goal-line.

The «gap» between the attacking player and defending players may vary depending on situation, but basically should be such that in case of sending the ball at the attacking player's foot one of defending players can play on the interception or tackle at the moment of opponent's reception of the ball.

Second. While performing a pass at the attacking player's foot one of attacking players, anticipating the moment and the direction of a pass, should abruptly go at the attacking player to intercept the ball or attack the opponent at reception of the ball, while another should drift towards the point, where the partner was situated before the moment of going at the attacking player. It should be the defending player, in whose «zone of responsibility» the attacking player tries to come over the ball, who goes at the attacking player.

Third. If the attacking player begins to move for reception of the ball into space behind the back of the defending player, while the attacking player's partner is ready to pass the ball on his way, both defending players should begin to move back to eliminate a possibility of attacking player receiving the ball.

Fourth. To press the attacking player without the ball out towards the half-way line, defending players should move around at some distance towards the half-way line and catch him offside, from whence the last will be forced to go back to space between defending players and the goal-line of the attacking team.

Moving forward may be performed by defending players at the moment when the ball cannot be sent by an opponent towards the goal-line of the defending team.

Fifth. The availability of a player from the attacking team possessing the ball to send the ball to a partner who begins to move into the space behind the defending player's back answers for a signal for defending players to begin to move back while pressing the attacking player out towards the half-way line.

For notes

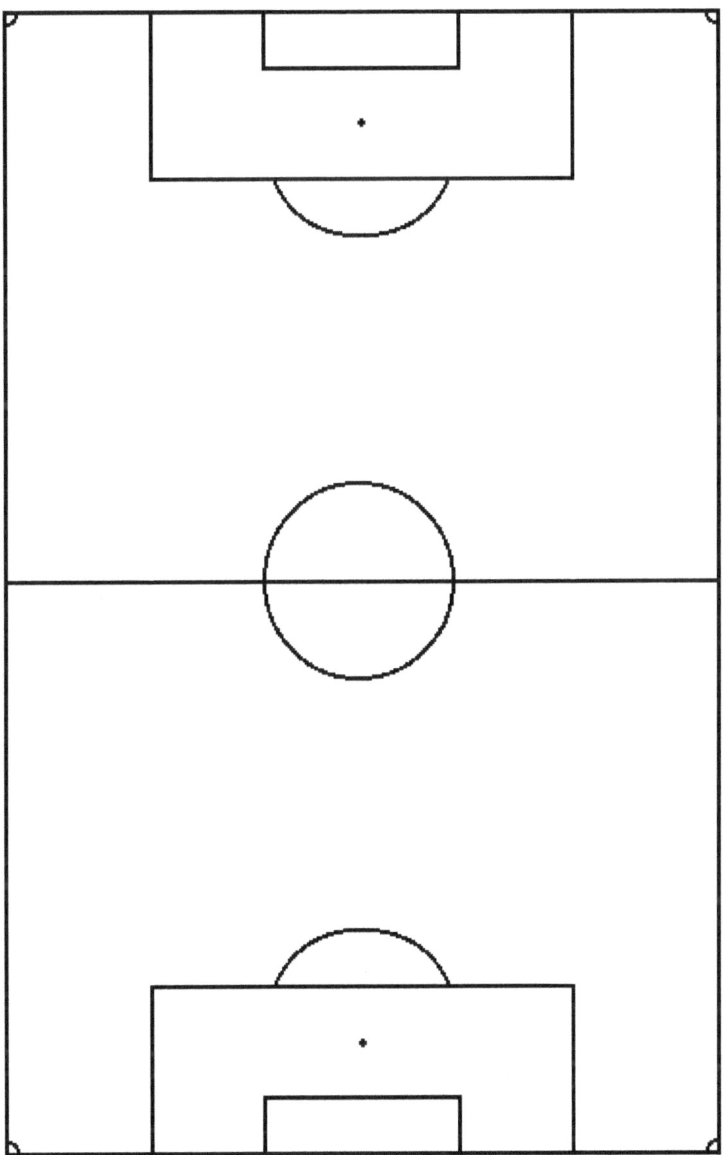

CHAPTER 4. DEFENDING PLAYERS' ACTIONS IN «TWO ON ATTACKING PLAYER MOVING WITH THE BALL TOWARDS THEM ALONG THE LENGTH OF THE PITCH» SITUATIONS

Introduction

On course of the game there may occur situations, when the player from the attacking team succeeds in coming over the ball in area situated along the length of the pitch at front of two defending players of the same «play line», situated roughly in parallel to each other across the width of the pitch at 8-10 meters with the zonal method of defensive play.

Further on this player may perform a shot on goal or a pass depending on the position and actions of partners, and also may try to deliver the ball using dribbling into the area behind these two defending players' back.

If the attacking player begins to move with the ball towards two defending players with a view to get into the area behind their back, when two defending players' actions in these situations ultimately come down to tackling or knocking the ball out from an opponent.

Successful performance of tackling or knocking the ball out by them suggests:

– well-timed approach of one of defending players with the attacking player and realization of attempt to tackle or knock the ball out from him;

– covering by the second defending player of a partner to tackle or knock the ball out from the attacking player, if a partner fails to do that.

These actions of defending players in «two on the attacking player moving with the ball towards them along the length of the pitch» may be performed both in defensive line and midfield and attacking lines with the zonal pressing.

Two defending players' actions against the attacking player moving with the ball towards them along the length of the pitch

Solving the issue of delivering the ball into space behind defending players' back, the attacking players may act as follows:

– try to go with the ball between two defending players (fig. 21A);

– outplay one of defending players from side opposite to where another defending player is situated (fig. 21B);

– send the ball past one of defending players or above him into space behind his back, and then quickly move to the ball, going this defending player round from the right or left side (fig. 21C).

In cases when the attacking player with the ball moves towards two defending players (right and left) with a view to deliver the ball using dribbling into space behind their back, defending players' actions are as follows.

Defending player, in whose «zone of responsibility» the attacking player with the ball moves, gets ready to face the opponent, slightly coming to the fore, to be able to tackle or knock the ball out at the right moment after getting closer to him.

Getting ready to tacking or knocking the ball out and beginning to perform these actions, this defending player should eliminate a possibility of attacking player going with the ball towards through space, located on the side opposite to where the second defending player is situated, and create apparently favorable conditions for the attacking player to cross the line of defensive players through the space between them.

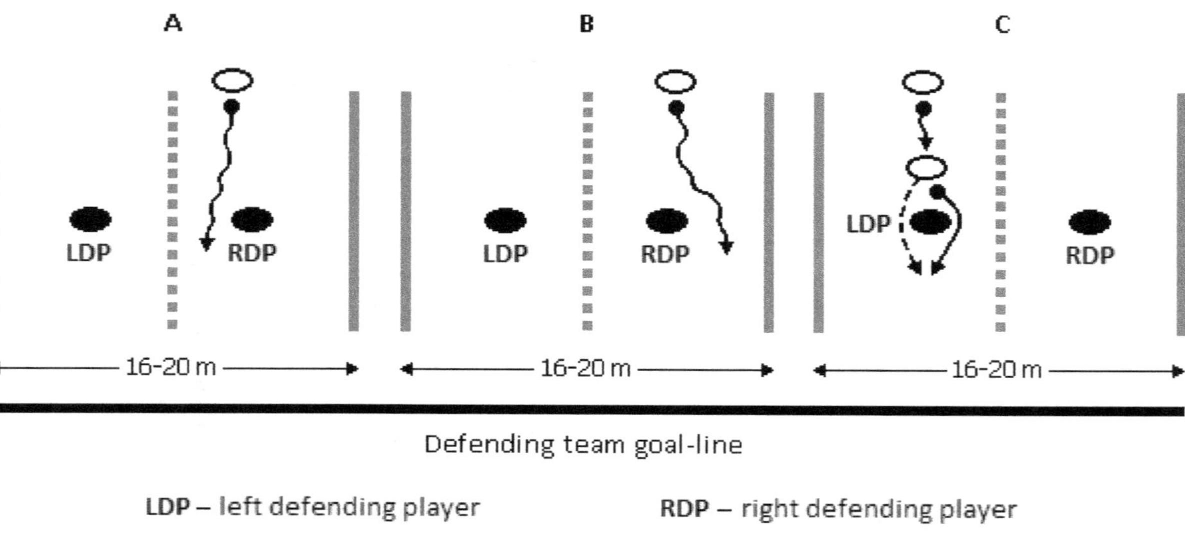

Fig. 21. Possible actions of the attacking player having come over the ball in area at front of two defending players along the length of the pitch at attempts to deliver the ball individually into space behind defending players' back

To this effect the defending player should bear in mind solution of a problem to provoke the attacking player to move with the ball towards the second defending player both while performing preparative actions to tackling and knocking out the ball and while beginning of attempt to tackle or knock the ball out.

While one of defending players gets ready to accomplish a tackle or knocking the ball out, another begins to move towards partner. He moves so that to be 3-4 meters across the width and 1-2 meters along the length of the pitch closer than the defending player to own goal-line, i.e. diagonally to the partner relative to the goal-line, by the moment when the attacking player begins the performance of outplaying the defending player who closes with him first (fig. 22).

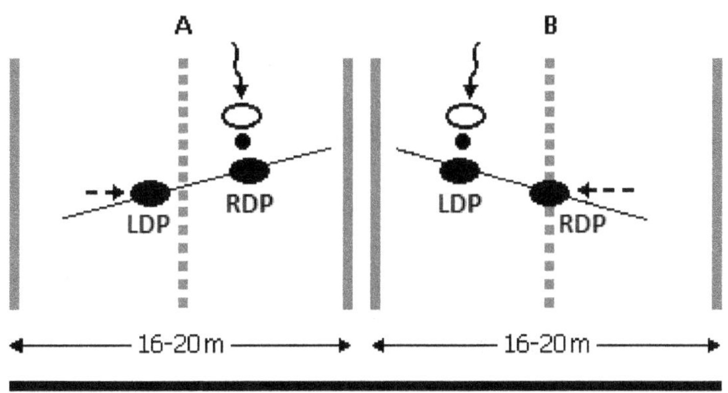

Fig. 22. Diagonal position of two defending players relative to the goal-line by the moment when the attacking player begins the performance of outplaying of defending player who closes with him first, at attempts to deliver the ball by the attacking player individually into space behind defending players' back

Above-described actions of defending players in cases of its timely performance should result in following:

– if the defending player, who closes with the attacking player first, fails to tackle or knock the ball out from him, when attacking player is forced to «stumble» upon the second defending player, who should tackle of knock the ball out from the opponent (fig. 23A);

– if the attacking player is able to outplay the defending player facing him first, from the side opposite to where the second defending player is situated, when the last can cover the partner, as at this moment he is situated, moving, a little closer to his goal-line than him (fig. 23B).

Resume

Successful performance of tacking or knocking the ball out from the attacking player, who is trying to deliver the ball into space behind their back using dribbling, by two defending players suggests the following kinds of actions.

First. The defending player, in whose «zone of responsibility» the attacking player with the ball moves, faces the opponent first.

Getting ready to tacking or knocking the ball out and beginning to perform these actions, this defending player should eliminate a possibility of attacking player going with the ball towards through space, located on the side opposite to where the second defending player is situated, and provoke the attacking player to move towards the second defending player.

Second. While the defending player, who faces the attacking player first, gets ready to accomplish a tackle or knocking the ball out, the second one begins to move towards partner.

He moves so that to be 3-4 meters across the width and 1-2 meters along the length of the pitch closer than the defending player to own goal-line, i.e. diagonally to the partner relative to the goal-line, by the moment when the attacking player begins the performance of outplaying the defending player who closes with him first.

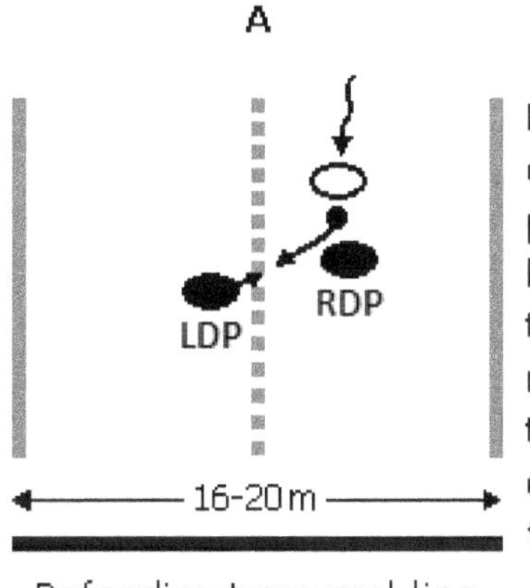

If the defending player closing with the attacking player first fails to tackle or knock the ball out from him, then the attacking player moving with the ball towards the second defending player is forced to stumble on him

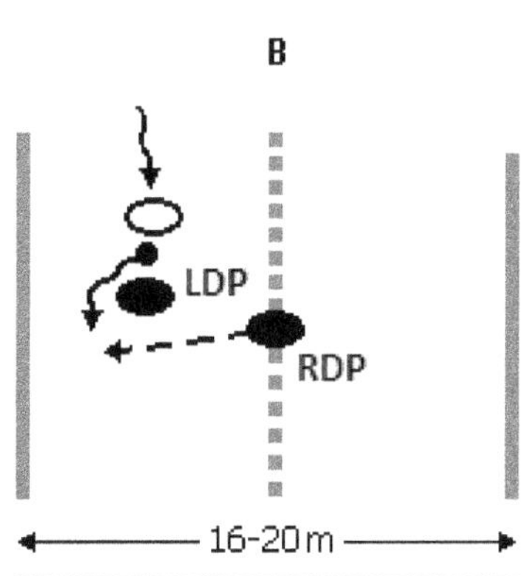

If the attacking player ia able to outplay the defending player who meets him first from the side opposite to where the second defending player is situated, the last may cover the partner and tackle or knock the ball out from the opponent, because he is situated little closer to his goal-line, than his partner, and on the move

LDP – left defending player
RDP – right defending player

Fig. 23. Possible scenarios with proper actions of two defending players at the attacking player's attempts to deliver the ball individually into space behind their back

Third. If the defending player, who faces the attacking player first, is not able to tackle or knock the ball out from him, this has to be done by the second defending player, because:

– the attacking player «stumbles» upon him while trying to go with the ball forward through the space between two defending players;

– the has a possibility to cover the partner, when the attacking player succeeds in outplaying the defending player who faces him first, from the side opposite to where the second defending player is situated.

For notes

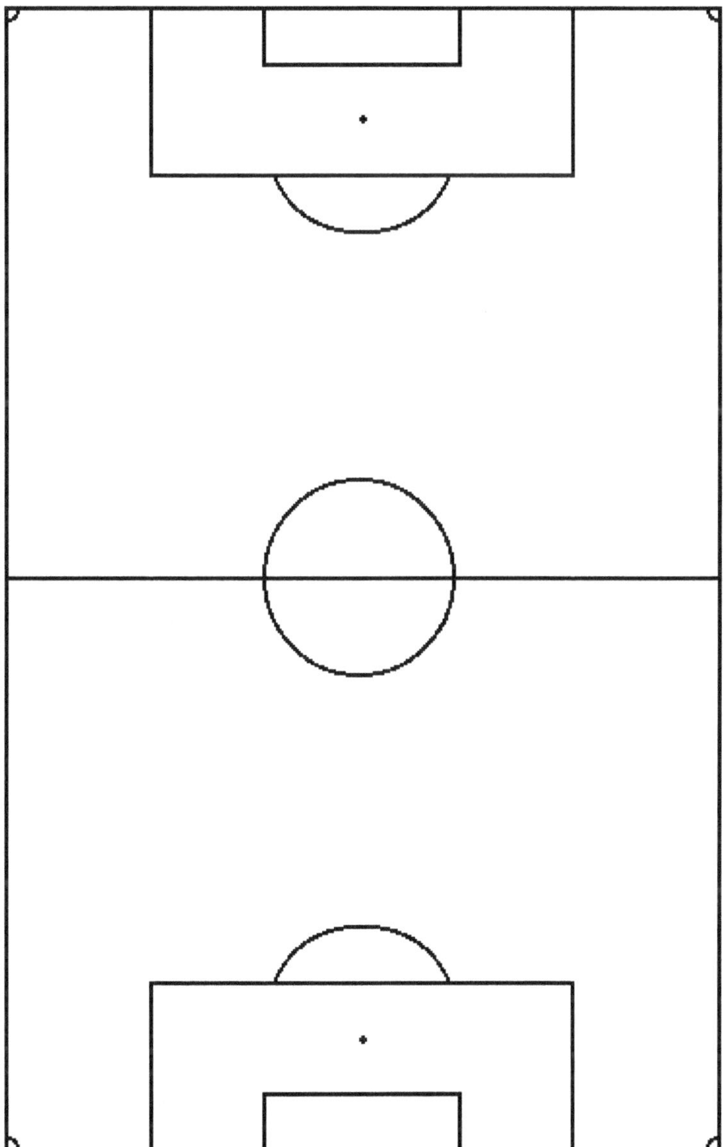

CHAPTER 5. DEFENDING PLAYERS' ACTIONS IN «TWO ON ATTACKING PLAYERS WITHOUT THE BALL SITUATED BETWEEN THEM ALONG THE LENGTH OF THE PITCH» SITUATIONS

Introduction

One of the typical is the play situation, when player from the attacking team without the ball is situated in space between two players from the defending team from different «play lines» along the length of the pitch, for example between the defender and midfielder or between the midfielder and forward.

This attacking player's actions of possessing the ball may come down to attempts to receive it at foot in space in front of the defending player, situated closer to his goal-line (defender of a back line) or behind his back (on a way).

Considering this situation it may be noted it includes «one defending player on attacking player without the ball, situated in front of him along the length of the pitch» play episode, plus one defending player, situated closer to the opponent's goal-line (defender of a front line).

In this regard two defending players' tactics of play in «two defending players on attacking player without the ball, situated between them across the length of the pitch» situations suggests performance of actions exercised in «one defending player on attacking player without the ball» situations by one of them (those who is situated closer to his goal-line). These actions include:

– controlling an opponent in «one's zone of responsibility»;

– restraint of his attempts to receive the ball in space in front of the defending player (at foot) and behind him (on a way).

Actions of defending player of a front line in «two defending players on attacking player without the ball, situated between them along the length of the pitch» situations depend on where the ball is sent to the attacking player (at foot or on a way), and come down to:

– tackling or knocking the ball out from the attacking player from the side of the opponent's goal-line, if the attacking player tries to receive the ball at foot;

– moving towards his goal-line for keeping the necessary distance between himself and a partner (a compact arrangement) and picking the ball up, if the attacking player tries to receive the ball on his way.

Two defending players' actions while controlling the attacking player without the ball, situated between them along the length of the pitch

If the attacking player without the ball appears in space between two players from the defending team of different «play lines» along the length of the pitch, when the defending player of a back line provides control of this player in own «zone of responsibility» 8-10 meters wide.

To this effect he locates 3-4 meters from the attacking player between him and his goal-line and also move at his local movements across the width and along the length of the pitch, trying to keep this distance and his opponent in front of him, situating face or half-sideways to opponent's goal-line.

Relative to the position of the defending player of a front line in considering situation the following should be noted. Basically he should be situated at a relatively short distance from the partner, as the sufficient efficiency of defensive play may be achieved when position of defending team players of different «play lines» provides required density of their location relative to each other along the length of the pitch.

Depending on area in which defending players are situated, on the attacking player without the ball movements and the distance between the attacking player and his partner possessing the ball at the moment, the distance between defending players may vary from 8-10 to 13-15 meters (fig. 24).

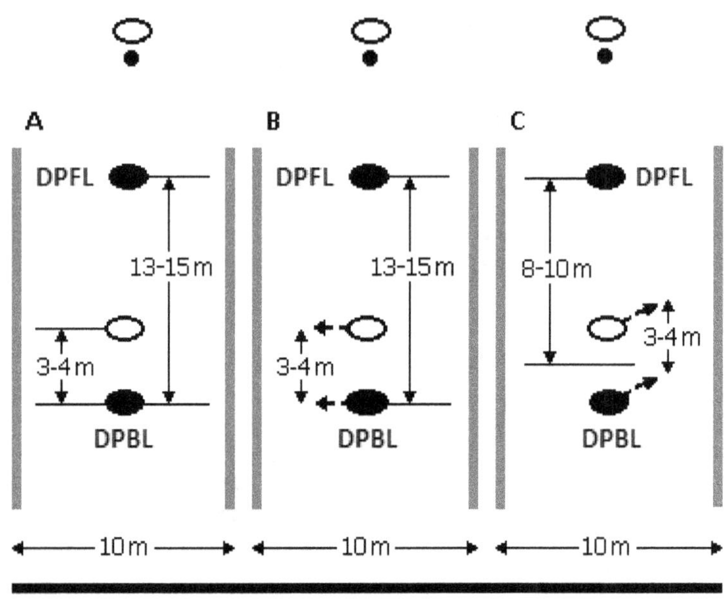

Fig. 24. Two defending players from different «play lines» position and actions while controlling the attacking player without the ball situated between them along the length of the pitch

Two defending players' actions while performing a pass at the attacking player's foot

While sending the ball at the attacking player's foot actions of the defending player situated closer to his goal-line are similar to those performed in «one on the attacking player without the ball» situations.

He abruptly goes at the attacking player and tries to intercept the ball or attack the opponent at reception of the ball, anticipating the moment and the direction of sending of the ball and entering into physical contact with him within the rules.

Acting in such a manner the defending player, unless intercepting the ball, forces the attacking player to turn towards or sideways to his goal-line, let the ball go from him while receiving it and consequently worsen control of play situation, begin to move with the ball towards his goal-line or back and to the side in conditions of physical contact.

Defending player situated closer to the opponent's goal-line acts in this situation as following.

In case of unsuccessful attempt to intercept the ball, sent to the attacking player over the pitch surface or on air, he turns his face towards his goal-line at once and begin to move quickly directly at the attacking player with a view to tackle or knock the ball out from him, after the ball crosses the line of his position along the length of the pitch.

Above-described actions of two defending players of different «play lines» in cases of its timely performance should result in following.

The attacking player situated between defending players along the length of the pitch and trying to come over the ball sent at his foot, appears to be «squeezed in a vise» by these players from two sides: from the side of the defending team goal-line and the attacking team goal-line (fig. 25).

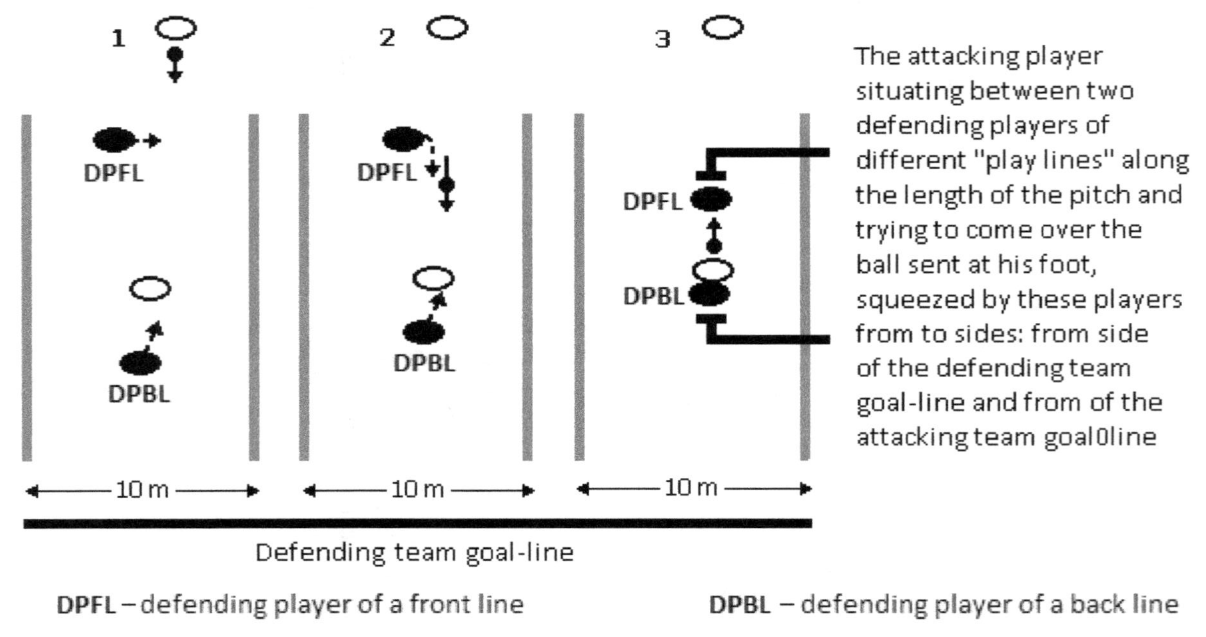

Fig. 25. Actions of two defending players of different «play lines» while performing a pass at the attacking player's foot, which player is situated between them along the length of the pitch

If the ball sent at the attacking player's foot, which player is situated between two defending players of different «play lines» along the length of the pitch, crosses the line of the defending player's front position, while this defending player begins to control of the attacking player's partners (fig. 26A) or move into space behind the defending player of a back line for covering his partner (fig. 26B), instead of moving directly at the attacking player, then such actions are incorrect in terms of zonal pressing.

This is due to the fact that in these cases space for attacking player with the ball actions is not limited from the side of the attacking team goal-line, and he has much more chances to come over the ball and continue actions with it.

In relatively scattered space this player can get rid of marking from the defending player who presses him, for example by performing some dummies and moving with the ball in various direction (back or back and to the side).

Two defending players' actions while performing a pass on the attacking player's way

If the attacking player begins to open for receiving the ball into space behind the back of the defending player of a back line, this defending player acts identically to how it goes in «one defending player on the attacking player without the ball» situations.

Having timely responded to the beginning of the attacking player's movement, he begins to move towards his goal-line and tries to keep the «gap» between the opponent and himself of 3-4 meters before the moment of sending the ball to the attacking player. Until the defending player identifies the direction of the ball sent on the attacking player's way, he moves back so that to see both attacking player without the ball and his partner possessing the ball.

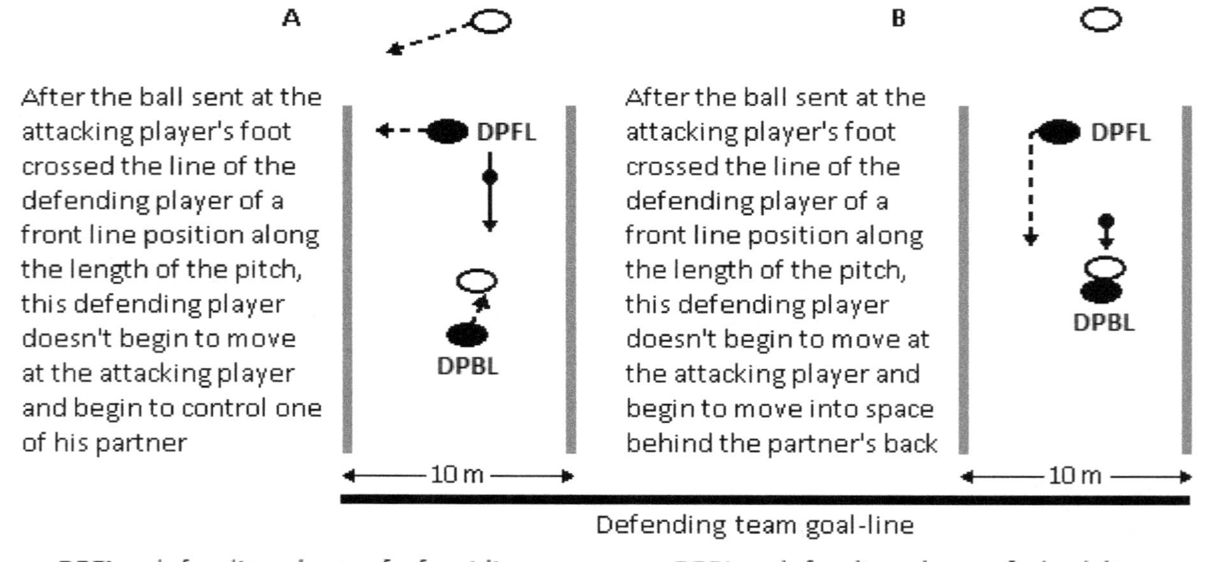

Fig. 26. Wrong in terms of zonal pressing actions of defending player of a front line while performing a pass at the attacking player's foot, which player is situated between two defending players along the length of the pitch

While observing these conditions by the defending player generally not only the possibility of attacking player receiving the ball in case of a pass on a way is excluded, and even situations then it depends on speed performance of defending and attacking players, who will come over the ball sent into space behind the defending player's back, do not occur.

If the defending player of a back line acts properly in situation, when the attacking player begins to move for receiving the ball into space behind his back, then distance between defending players of different «play lines» will increase, i.e. a compact arrangement of their position along the length of the pitch will be broken.

Therefore in this situation, when a pass on the attacking player's way has followed, the defending player of a front line should begin to move towards his goal-line directly after the ball crosses the line of his position along the length of the pitch, if he fails to intercept the ball (fig. 27).

The distance of defending player of a front line move back varies depending on situation, but generally should be such, that he should be on the ball first (can pick-up the ball) in cases when the defending player of a back line play it out into space between two defending players along the length of the pitch.

Actions of the defending player of a front line may be considered wrong in terms of zonal pressing, if he doesn't move towards his goal-line, having failed to intercept the ball sent on the attacking player's way (fig. 28).

Breach of a compact arrangement of defending players along the length of the pitch results in formation of uncontrolled space, which size is determined by distance of the defending player of a back line move back.

In cases of playing the ball out into this space by the defending player of a back line, that often occurs at passes on the attacking player's way with a mount trajectory, players from the attacking team get the opportunity to perform picking-up the ball first.

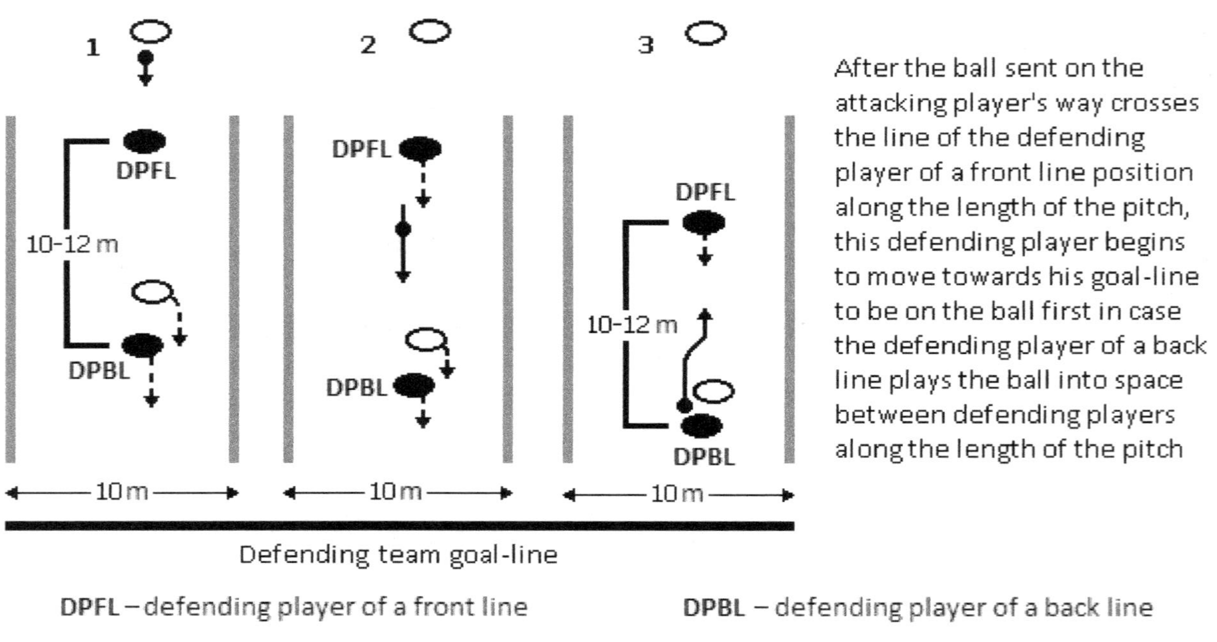

Fig. 27. Actions of the defending player of a front line while performing a pass on the attacking player's way into space behind the back of the defending player of a back line

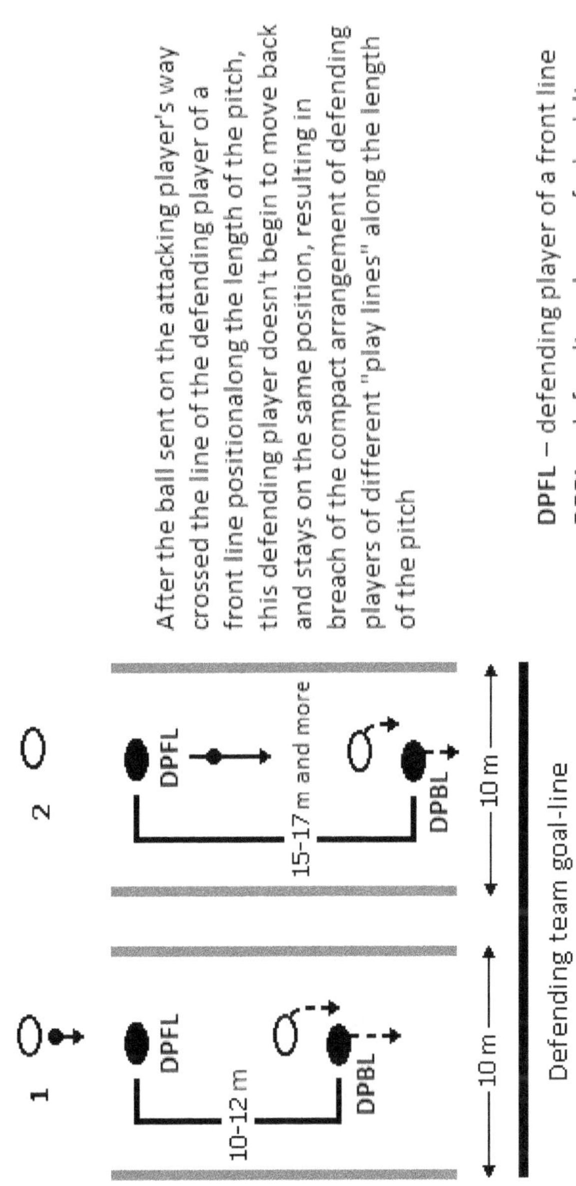

Fig. 28. Wrong in terms of zonal pressing actions of the defending player of a front line while performing a pass on the attacking player's way into space behind the back of the defending player

Resume

Specificity of two defending players' actions in «two on the attacking player without the ball, situated between them along the length of the pitch», is due to that in these cases players of different «play lines» interact.

Their actions success in these situations depends on observing several conditions.

First. While controlling the attacking player without the ball defending players should be situated at relatively short distance from each other for observing necessary compact arrangement along the length of the pitch (from 8-10 meters to 13-15 meters depending on situation).

Second. While the ball is sent at the attacking player's foot, defending players should vice the opponent through following actions:

– the defending players of a back line abruptly goes at the attacking player and tries to intercept the ball or attack the opponent at reception of the ball, anticipating the moment and the direction of sending of the ball and entering into physical contact with him;

– after the ball has crossed the line of his position, the defending player of a front line turn his face towards his goal-line and quickly move directly at the attacking player.

Third. If the attacking player begins to open for receiving the ball into space behind the back of the defending player of a back line, this player moves towards his goal-line, having timely responded to the beginning of the attacking player's movement, and tries to keep the «gap» between the opponent and himself of 3-4 meters before the moment of sending the ball to the opponent.

Fourth. While sending the ball on the attacking player's way into space behind the back of the defending player of a front line, the defending player of a front line should move towards his goal-line after the ball crosses the line of his position to keep a compact arrangement of defending players' position along the length of the pitch, if he fails to intercept the ball.

For notes

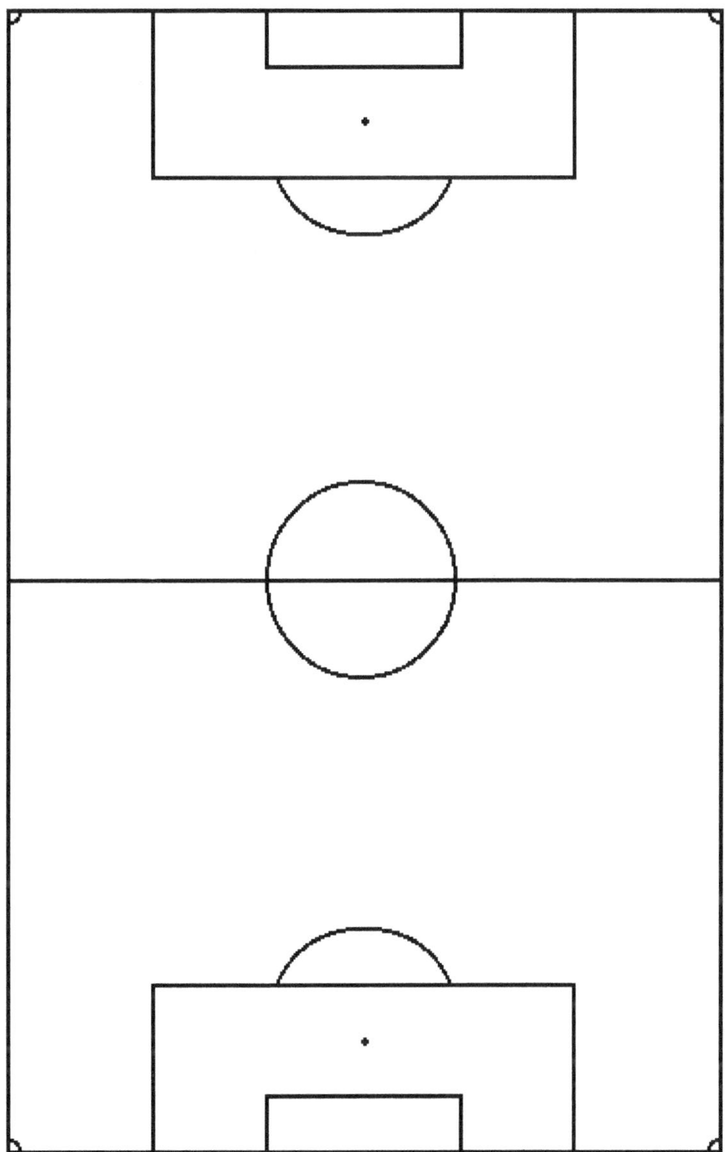

AFTERWORD

First. In matches of teams applying zonal pressing, regardless of tactical schemes of play construction, there are following kinds of typical local actions while performing defending actions:

– «one defending player on attacking player without the ball situated in front of him along the length of the pitch»;

– «two defending players on attacking player without the ball situated in front of them along the length of the pitch»;

– «two defending players on attacking player moving with the ball towards them along the length of the pitch»;

– «two defending players on attacking player without the ball situated between them along the length of the pitch».

Second. Since individual actions and interactions of two defending players in each of typical local situations are the same with different tactical schemes of play construction by teams using zonal pressing, these actions are basic elements of zonal pressing tactics.

Third. Defending players' actions and interactions in each of typical local situation while applying zonal pressing are completely different than while using man to man marking.

If while man to man marking every defending player is responsible only for the certain player from the attacking team, then during the zonal pressing it is necessary for them to anticipate actions of the attacking player situated in their «zone of responsibility» and the attacking player possessing the ball at the same time, and to correlate their opportunities to act in concert at a time.

In this regard the defensive play with the zonal pressing requires from footballers the ability to anticipate development of situations (reactions of higher anticipation level), on one hand, and provides them with the possibility to constantly improve these ability, defining the level of tactical prowess, on another, to much higher degree than during man to man marking.

Fourth. Footballers' knowledge of how to act and interact in typical local situations with the involvement of one or two defending players during the zonal pressing offers an opportunity to the team to perform zonal pressing in the context of different tactical schemes of play construction.

Fifth. Defensive actions and interactions in typical local situations with the involvement of one or two defending players as basic elements of zonal pressing tactics should be trained intentionally using special drills, firstly by footballers of child and youth level.

BIBLIOGRAPHY

Аверьянов А. Характеристика варианта зонного метода обороны с четырьмя защитниками // Теория и практика футбола. – 2003. – № 2. – С. 2-6.

Ано Г. Новый этап в развитии футбола. Игра с четырьмя защитниками // Спортивные игры. – 1956. – № 7. – С. 21-23.

Аркадьев Б.А. Тактика «подвижной обороны» / В книге: Тактика футбольной игры. – М.: Физкультура и спорт, 1962. – С. 68-75.

Голомазов С., Чирва Б. Какая защита надежнее? / Футбол. Арифметика тактики: Методические разработки для слушателей ВШТ. Выпуск 8. – М., РГАФК, 1998. – С. 7-11.

Гомельский А. Игра в защите / В книге: Тактика баскетбола. – М.: Физкультура и спорт, 1966. – С. 34-86.

Джоунз Р., Трэнтер Т. Футбол. Тактика защиты и нападения (пер. с англ.). – М.: ТВТ Дивизион, 2008. – 132 с.

Зар Р. Прессинг. Система защиты национальной баскетбольной сборной Италии // Спортивные игры. – 1956. – № 1. – С. 14.

Игнатьев Б. Разные лица либеро // Еженедельник «Футбол». – № 9. – 1996. – С. 7-8.

Игнатьева В.Я. Тактика защиты / В книге: Гандбол: Пособие для институтов физической культуры. – М.: Физкультура и спорт, 1983. – С. 57-67.

Калинин А. Игра защитников. – М.: Физкультура и спорт, 1967. – 78 с.

Качалин Г.Д. Игра защитников / В книге: Тактика футбола. – М.: Физкультура и спорт, 1986. – С. 41-50.

Клесов И., Лексаков А., Российский С. Вопросы организации зонной обороны при игре «четыре защитника в линию» // Теория и практика футбола. – 2004. – № 4. – С. 2-5.

Костка В. Зонный прессинг / В книге: Современный хоккей (перевод с чешского Б.Г. Байгозина). – М.: Физкультура и спорт, 1976. – С. 174-188.

Кунст-Германеску И. Зонная защита / В книге: Ручной мяч 7:7 (сокращенный перевод с румынского В.И. Чоговадзе). – М.: Физкультура и спорт, 1969. – С. 112-114.

Лаверс К. Действия игроков в обороне в ситуации «один в один» / В книге: Пособие для футбольных тренеров. – М.: Фонд «Национальная академия футбола, 2007. – С. 250-253.

Левитанус М.С. «Зона» имеет право на жизнь // Советский спорт. – 2 декабря 1960.

Люкези М. Футбол. Обучение системе игры 4-3-3 (пер. с англ.). – М.: ТВТ Дивизион, 2008. – 164 с.

Михелс Р. Построение команды: путь к успеху. – Киев: Центр лицензирования Федерации футбола Украины, 2006. – 224 с.

Морозов С. Анализ зонного метода обороны при игре «в четыре защитника» // Футбол-Профи. – Донецк (Украина). – 2006. – № 1 (2). – С. 16-19.

Семашко Н.В., Цетлин П.М. Системы защиты / В книге: Обучение и тренировка баскетбольных команд. – М.: Изд. военного министерства СССР, 1950. – С. 66-72.

Стонкус С. Секреты зонного прессинга // Спортивные игры. – 1966. – № 6. – С. 11.

Тактика защиты / В книге: Баскетбол: Учебник для институтов физической культуры. Изд. 2-е, переработанное // Под ред. Н.В. Семашко. – М.: Физкультура и спорт, 1976. – С. 98-120.

Тактика игры / В книге: Футбол: Учебник для институтов физической культуры // Под ред. М.С. Полишкиса и В.А. Выжгина. – М.: Физкультура, образование и наука, 1999. – С. 52-89.

Футбол. Правила игры 2011 г. – М., 2011. – 71 с.

Чирва Б. Суть и принципиальные отличия тактики действий обороняющегося игрока при персональной опеке, «закрытии зоны» и индивидуальном зонном прессинге // Теория и практика футбола. – 2002. – № 1. – С. 2-7.

Чирва Б. Величина игрового пространства, которое могут перекрыть футболисты при разном расположении, как предпосылка к выбору тактики игры в обороне // Теория и практика футбола. – 2002. – № 3. – С. 2-6.

Чирва Б. Основы зонного прессинга: принцип действий обороняющихся игроков в ситуациях «один против атакующего игрока без мяча» // Теория и практика футбола. – 2004. – № 3. – С. 2-9.

Чирва Б. Двое против атакующего игрока без мяча, находящегося между ними по длине поля // «Футбол-Профи». – Донецк (Украина), 2006. – № 2 (3). – С. 26-31.

Чирва Б.Г. Основы зонного прессинга: действия обороняющихся игроков в ситуациях «двое против атакующего игрока без мяча, находящегося перед ними по длине поля» // Футбол-Профи. – Донецк (Украина). – 2006. – № 4 (5).

Чирва Б.Г. Организация оборонительных действий в системе зонного прессинга в футболе // Вестник Московского университета МВД России. – 2007. – № 5. – С. 162-164.

Чирва Б.Г. Футбол. Концепция технической и тактической подготовки футболистов. – 2-е изд., перераб. и доп. 39 / Б.Г. Чирва. – М.: ТВТ Дивизион, 2015. – 352 с.

Chirva Boris Grigorievich

Ph.D. in Physical Education, obtains coaching license grade «A», leading Russian soccer strategist. He was born in 1959 and lives in Moscow, Russia.

Previously he was a player of professional soccer teams in First and Second division of USSR championship.

After ending his soccer career he worked as a youth teams coach for eight years and cultivated a player – champion of USSR Under-16-17.

In 1992-93 he was educating in Russian Higher coaching school. Thereafter he began to work on scientific-methods. He passed Ph. D. defense on young players cultivation in 1997, and defended doctoral dissertation about «Basic and professional technical and tactical training of players» in 2008.

During 1999-2013 he was scientific consultant on training methods and worked as a coach in Russian Premier-league clubs. From 2006 till 2008 he worked in Abramovich's National academy of soccer foundation, where were engaged in professional development of Russian youth coaches and methodological support of youth soccer schools and academies.

At the moment he is an educator in Russian coaching license courses in grades «B», «A» and «PRO».

Currently he has published 170 scientific-methods works on various issues of professional and young players training, including 24 monographs, and also he is an author of two training films about players training.

The main direction of his creative activity today is the continuation of work on creation of «Theory and methods of world soccer» in 5 sections: training of soccer technique, preparation and play of professional teams, preparation and play of goalkeepers, soccer strategy and tactic, cultivation of young players.

www.ingramcontent.com/pod-product-compliance
Lightning Source LLC
Chambersburg PA
CBHW071844020426
42331CB00007B/1842

9785987241912